This

Sandra Lee
semi-homemade®

slow cooker recipes

book belongs to:

....

Meredith® Books Des Moines, Iowa

sem·i·home·made

adj. **1:** a stress-free solution-based formula that provides savvy shortcuts and affordable, timesaving tips for overextended do-it-yourself homemakers **2:** a quick and easy equation wherein 70% ready-made convenience products are added to 30% fresh ingredients with creative personal style, allowing homemakers to take 100% of the credit for something that looks, feels, or tastes homemade **3:** a foolproof resource for having it all—and having the time to enjoy it **4:** a method created by Sandra Lee for home, garden, crafts, beauty, food, fashion, and entertaining wherein everything looks, tastes, and feels as if it was made from scratch.

Solution-based **E**nterprise that **M**otivates, **I**nspires, and **H**elps **O**rganize and **M**anage time, while **E**nriching **M**odern life by **A**dding **D**ependable shortcuts **E**very day.

dedications

To Hilary Lentini and Pamela Acuff
for always being quick to lend a heaping helping hand
and for the use of their very own slow cookers—
even if mulled Merlot is all that bubbles in them.

special thanks

To my Meredith family
Jack, Bob, Doug, Jim, Jan, Ken, Jeff, Mick, and Jessica

and

To my family from the Food Network
Brooke, Bob, Irene, Judy, Kathleen, and Eric.
What a great potluck finding you!

acknowledgments

A heartfelt thanks to my
not-so-slow cookin' team
Jeff: Culinary Director
Michael, Mark, Lisa, Laurent,
Pamela, Linda, and Valerie

Table of Contents

Chapter 1
One-Pot Wonders
16

Chapter 3
Casseroles
70

Chapter 2
Five-Ingredient Dishes
44

Chapter 4
Pasta, Rice & Risotto
102

Letter from Sandra

The slow cooker is back—and in a big way! The darling of a new generation of hip homemakers is making slow cooking cool all over again. Whether you work at home or work in the office, slow cooking the Semi-Homemade® way is about as prep-free as you're going to find. Go ahead, live your life! Your meal cooks for you while you are out running errands, spending time with loved ones, or unwinding after a busy day.

While some of us traded in our crockery cookers for microwaves, others kept right on slow cooking. I was reintroduced to its possibilities by my friend Hilary, a busy working mom with a husband and two small daughters. We were sitting down to work one morning when her young daughter raced into the room and screeched to a stop, exclaiming, "What's for dinner?" At 9:00 in the morning! And sure enough, the lemony smell of chicken was wafting through the house, mingling with the cinnamon scent of our coffee. Hilary tossed in chicken breasts, lemon, oregano, and a can of stewed tomatoes at breakfast and left the slow cooker to cook all day while she went about her regular routine. High tech has its place, but the slow cooker cooks when you can't.

Of course, there are shelf after shelf of slow cooker books on the market. I looked through them and realized—all that prep work can take forever! Slow cooking isn't fast at all if you have to chop mounds of vegetables, sear meat, or add endless ingredients. So I set out to make slow cooking super simple the Semi-Homemade® way. Just pair 70% store-bought products with 30% fresh ingredients and a pinch of your own ingenuity to create dishes with 100% made-from-scratch flavor. Using prechopped vegetables and packaged broth, even precooked meat, shortens prep time, letting you serve delicious meals without spending hours in the kitchen. Just dump everything in, cover, and come home to a hot, healthy meal that's ready to serve when you're ready to eat.

Slow cooking adapts to our lifestyle, whatever it might be. Some of us, like Hilary, use our slow cookers almost every day. Others, like my friend Pamela bring out theirs to mull wine during the holidays, simmer meatballs for parties, or win fans over with some before-the-game chili. My friend Jeff is the goodie guru, who taught me how to bake fast and fabulous in the slow cooker without a special "insert" basket. This book satisfies all appetites, whether you're looking to feed the family, entertain a crowd, or please a party of just one. There are soups for the soul and desserts for the sweet tooth. There are trendy chicken du jour; light, tender pastas; and rich, hearty meats. There are budget-conscious meals and health-conscious dinners; there are even one-pot wonders when you want it all in one, as well as five-ingredient meals that turn a little into a lot of flavor. As a bonus, I've even included a chapter of fabulously retro casseroles—quick to make and quicker to slide in the oven.

That '70s crockery cooker may be the comeback kid of the kitchen, but saving time and eating well are always in style. Prep fast, cook slow, live life—the Semi-Homemade® way.

Cheers to healthy, happy slow cooking!

Sue

Sandra Lee

Choosing a Slow Cooker

Low   High

Off   Warm

So many slow cookers, so little time! With all the sizes, shapes, colors, designs, and styles, how can you pick the right one for your family? Read on for some simple tips for fabulous food.

Cooker Sizes and Styles

Totable slow cooker: Say good-bye to the days of trying to transport the very "untransportable" slow cooker! With the new totable device (photo, bottom left) food can be cooked to perfection, then carried to potlucks and parties with ease. Just slip the safety catches for the lid in place and snap the magnetized handles together for piping hot, portable food.

Small cookers: Not everybody needs to prepare mass quantities of slow-cooked food. For single people, couples, and party appetizers, the 1½-quart cooker is the best option. For couples (who want leftovers) and small families, choose a 3½- to 4½-quart cooker. This size is perfect for soups, stews, and chilies.

Large cookers: Most of the recipes in this book call for larger cookers, between 4 and 5 quarts. This size works well for everyone because large families have plenty to eat and small families and couples will have enough leftovers to freeze. For super-large families, 6- to 8-quart slow cookers are available (photo, page 8).

Slow Cooker Savvy

Keep these hints in mind when it comes to slow cooker success:

Slow cookers work best when filled at least one-half full and not more than two-thirds full. Pay attention to the size of slow cooker called for in each recipe. Layer ingredients as directed in the recipes or follow manufacturer's directions.

Never put frozen meat in a slow cooker; thaw it first. Browning meat such as roasts and chops is a preference, not a necessity. If you're short on time, skip the skillet and go straight to the slow cooker.

Be careful not to peek too often! Each time you open the lid, another 15 minutes must be added to your cooking time.

Large and small cookers

Totable cooker

From Stovetop to Slow Cooker

Grandma's famous chili is tops, but can it be adapted to the slow cooker? Of course! With a few simple tweaks, most recipes are perfect candidates for slow cooker make-overs.

Recipe Conversion

Soups, chilies, and stews (as well as many other recipes) can be adapted from stovetop to slow cooker easily. Here are some great guidelines:

Meat selection: Start with meat that is less tender, such as beef chuck or pork blade roast. Slow, moist cooking will soften the meat fibers and make tough meat tender and juicy. Trim the meat and, if desired, brown it in a skillet.

Find a recipe: Look through this book to find a recipe similar to the one you would like to adapt (for example, if you want to slow cook your favorite chili recipe, check out Five-Alarm Three-Bean Chili on page 199). Then use it as a guide for quantities, piece sizes, liquid amounts, and cooking times.

Cutting and arranging: Cut vegetables and other necessary ingredients into small, bite-size pieces so they cook uniformly and are easy to eat. When cooking larger cuts of meat, add the vegetables to the slow cooker first and top with the meat. This ensures that the vegetables are tender when the meat is done.

Adding liquid: Unless the recipe calls for long-grain rice, cut the amount of liquid by about half from the stovetop recipe (use the amount called for in the guide recipe you used from this book).

Fabulous Ingredients

Put good food in and good food will come out! Just remember that certain ingredients are better for long cooking—for example, root veggies (such as potatoes and carrots) are ideal.

Liquids

Converted rice

Meat

Herbs

The Right Stuff

There are certain foods that perform wonderfully in slow cookers, especially tough cuts of meat and firm vegetables.

Liquids such as broth, wine, and juices add much-needed moistness to slow cooking. They also supply tons of flavor to recipes.

Rice can be cooked in the slow cooker in certain recipes. Converted rice is your best bet for ideal texture.

Meat is a must in most (but not all!) slow cooker recipes. Tougher cuts of meat benefit the most from slow cooking.

Herbs are the ingredient that turn a dish from ho-hum to wow! When using fresh herbs, add them at the very end of cooking so they retain their flavor. Dried herbs can be added earlier in the cooking process. One-third the amount of a dried herb can be substituted for fresh—so if 1 tablespoon fresh is called for, 1 teaspoon of dried should be substituted in its place.

13

Extra-Easy Entertaining

The slow cooker is quite the party partner! It works well for cooking and warming cocktail party appetizers such as beverages, cheese dips, chicken wings, and cocktail meatballs.

The slow cooker is irreplaceable during the holiday celebrations. While the oven is packed with holiday fixin's, do double duty by popping a luscious dessert (such as Chianti Poached Pears) in the slow cooker and voilà! Perfection!

One-Pot Wonders

My friend Pamela still has her first slow cooker—a trusty harvest brown model stained burgundy inside from mulling wine every Christmas since 1979. Occasionally she drags it out to make meatballs, and people always comment on the hint of wine in the sauce. These days people use the slow cooker for just about anything—or everything. This chapter is filled with versatile recipes that cover all the courses, serving up soup, meat, and vegetables in one do-it-all dish. These singular sensations are anything but plain, blending a whirlwind of colors, textures, and flavors into exotic cuisine from Moroccan to Tex-Mex. Ham goes Hawaiian with pineapples and snap peas; smoked pork is Southern-style with dumplings and greens; veal feels oh-so-French with a tipple of white Zin and très chic red potatoes. It's hard to have it all. But cook an entire meal in one pot, and it suddenly seems easy.

The Recipes

Pot Roast with Mushroom Gravy

Prep 15 minutes
Cook LOW 8 to 10 hours
Makes 6 servings

1	pound red potatoes, cut into wedges
8	ounces baby carrots
1	package (8-ounce) presliced fresh mushrooms
1	onion, cut into 1-inch wedges through the core
2	ribs celery, sliced
3	pounds beef chuck roast
1	can (14-ounce) reduced-sodium beef broth, *Swanson*®
1	can (10-ounce) mushroom gravy, *Campbell's*®
1	packet (1.5-ounce) slow cooker beef stew seasoning mix, *McCormick*®

1. In a 5-quart slow cooker, combine potatoes, carrots, mushrooms, onion, and celery. Place roast on top of vegetables.

2. In a medium bowl, stir together beef broth, gravy, and beef stew seasoning mix. Pour over roast.

3. Cover and cook on LOW heat setting for 8 to 10 hours.

Swiss Steak with Wild Mushroom Barley

Prep 10 minutes
Cook LOW 8 to 10 hours
Makes 6 servings

1   package (8-ounce) presliced fresh mushrooms
1   cup frozen chopped onion, *Ore-Ida*®
½   cup pearl barley, *Arrowhead Mills*®
2   packages (0.5 ounce each) dried mushroom medley, *Melissa's*®
2½   pounds beef round steak 1 inch thick, cut into serving portions
4   cups reduced-sodium beef broth, *Swanson*®
1   can (10.75-ounce) condensed cream of mushroom soup, *Campbell's*®
1   envelope (1-ounce) onion soup mix, *Lipton*®
   Fresh thyme sprigs (optional)

1. In a 5-quart slow cooker, combine fresh mushrooms, onion, barley, and dried mushrooms. Place meat on top of vegetable mixture.

2. In a medium bowl, stir together beef broth, soup, and onion soup mix. Pour over meat.

3. Cover and cook on LOW heat setting for 8 to 10 hours.

4. Serve with thyme (optional).

Asian Short Ribs with Broccoli and Rice

Prep 10 minutes
Cook LOW 8 to 10 hours
Makes 6 servings

Light, healthy, and virtually prep-free, this Asian-style meal uses stir-fry seasoning and canned chicken broth to be ready at the drop of a chopstick. Buy fresh broccoli florets—they have more vitamins.

3   pounds beef short ribs
2   packets (1 ounce each) beef broccoli stir-fry seasoning mix, *Kikkoman*®
2   cans (14 ounces each) reduced-sodium chicken broth, *Swanson*®
1½   cups converted long-grain rice, *Uncle Ben's*®
1   cup water
1   bag (16-ounce) fresh broccoli florets, *Mann's*®

1. Sprinkle ribs with 1 packet of the stir-fry seasoning mix; set aside.

2. In a 5- to 6-quart slow cooker, combine chicken broth, rice, water, and the remaining stir-fry seasoning mix. Add ribs, bone sides down. Top with broccoli.

3. Cover and cook on LOW heat setting for 8 to 10 hours.

White Zinfandel-Braised Veal

Prep 15 minutes
Cook LOW 6 to 8 hours
Makes 4 servings

2   pounds veal shoulder chops
     Salt and ground black pepper
4   Yukon gold potatoes, cut into 1-inch wedges
1   large onion, cut into 1-inch wedges through the core
1   can (14.5-ounce) diced tomatoes with garlic, basil, and oregano, *S&W*®
1   can (10.75-ounce) condensed cream of potato soup, *Campbell's*®
1   cup white Zinfandel wine

1. Sprinkle chops with salt and pepper; set aside.

2. In a 5-quart slow cooker, combine potatoes and onion. Place chops on top of vegetables.

3. In a medium bowl, stir together undrained tomatoes, soup, and wine. Spoon over chops.

4. Cover and cook on LOW heat setting for 6 to 8 hours.

Lamb Shanks with White Beans

Prep 10 minutes
Cook LOW 10 to 12 hours
Makes 4 servings

4	1-pound lamb shanks
1½	teaspoons ground black pepper
1	teaspoon salt
2	cans (15 ounces each) cannellini beans, drained, *Progresso*®
1	can (14.5-ounce) diced tomatoes with garlic, basil, and oregano, *S&W*®
1½	cups white wine, Chardonnay
1	envelope (1-ounce) onion soup mix, *Lipton*®
2	teaspoons dried Italian seasoning, *McCormick*®
1	teaspoon bottled crushed garlic, *Christopher Ranch*®
	Fresh parsley sprigs (optional)

1. Trim off excess fat and silver skin from lamb shanks. Sprinkle with pepper and salt; set aside.

2. In a 5-quart slow cooker, stir together beans, undrained tomatoes, wine, onion soup mix, Italian seasoning, and garlic until thoroughly combined. Place lamb shanks on top of bean mixture.

3. Cover and cook on LOW heat setting for 10 to 12 hours.

4. Serve with parsley (optional).

Pork Roast with
Cabbage and Apples

Prep 15 minutes
Cook LOW 6 to 8 hours
Makes 6 servings

3	pounds pork shoulder roast
1	teaspoon ground black pepper
¾	teaspoon salt
¼	cup pickling spices, *Morton & Bassett*®
1	medium head green cabbage, cut into 2-inch wedges
1	pound new red potatoes, quartered
1	cup frozen chopped onion, *Ore-Ida*®
1	can (14-ounce) reduced-sodium chicken broth, *Swanson*®
1	cup dried apple slices, *Mariani*®

1. Sprinkle roast with pepper and salt; set aside. Cut a 6- to 8-inch square from a double thickness of 100%-cotton cheesecloth. Place pickling spices in center of cheesecloth square. Bring up corners of cheesecloth and tie closed with 100%-cotton string. Set aside.

2. In 5- to 6-quart slow cooker, arrange cabbage wedges. Top with roast, fat side up. Place cheesecloth bag, potatoes, and onion along sides of roast. Add chicken broth and arrange apple slices on top. Slow cooker will be full, but ingredients will cook down quickly.

3. Cover and cook on LOW heat setting for 6 to 8 hours.

Smoked Pork with Greens and Corn Bread Dumplings

Prep 15 minutes
Cook LOW 6 to 8 hours; plus 15 minutes on HIGH
Makes 6 servings

1	bag (16-ounce) precut collard greens, *Cut 'n Clean Greens*®
3	cans (14 ounces each) reduced-sodium chicken broth, *Swanson*®
1½	cups frozen chopped onion, *Ore-Ida*®
2	tablespoons cider vinegar, *Heinz*®
1	tablespoon sugar
1	tablespoon plus 1 teaspoon Montreal steak seasoning, *McCormick*®
¼	teaspoon liquid smoke, *Wright's*®
1	3-pound pork shoulder roast
	FOR DUMPLINGS:
1	package (6.5-ounce) corn muffin mix, *Betty Crocker*®
1	cup baking mix, *Bisquick*®
⅔	cup evaporated milk, *Carnation*®

1. Place greens in a 5-quart slow cooker; set aside. In a medium pot, combine chicken broth, onion, vinegar, sugar, 1 tablespoon of the steak seasoning, and liquid smoke. Bring to a boil. Pour over greens.

2. Sprinkle fat side of roast with remaining 1 teaspoon steak seasoning. Place roast on the top of the greens.

3. Cover and cook on LOW heat setting for 6 to 8 hours.

4. Transfer roast to a serving platter and tent with aluminum foil to keep warm. Reserve cooking liquid in slow cooker. Cover slow cooker; turn to HIGH heat setting.

5. For dumplings, prepare a stack of 8 paper towels; set aside. In a medium bowl, combine corn muffin mix, baking mix, and evaporated milk. Stir to form a soft dough. Remove lid from slow cooker and drop dough by spoonfuls into hot mixture. Place paper towel stack on top of slow cooker (to absorb moisture). Secure with lid. Cook for 15 minutes.

6. Slice roast and serve with dumplings and greens.

Pork Chops with Creamy Succotash

Prep 15 minutes
Cook LOW 5 to 7 hours
Makes 4 servings

4   center-cut pork chops, cut 1 inch thick
2   teaspoons salt-free all-purpose seasoning, *McCormick*®
1½   teaspoons garlic salt, *Lawry's*®
2   cups frozen loose-pack whole-kernel corn, *Birds Eye*®
2   cups frozen loose-pack cut green beans, *Birds Eye*®
2   cups frozen loose-pack cut okra, *Pictsweet*®
1   cup frozen chopped onion, *Ore-Ida*®
½   red bell pepper, finely chopped
1¼   cups reduced-sodium chicken broth, *Swanson*®
1   package (2.64-ounce) country gravy mix, *McCormick*®
     Fresh thyme sprigs (optional)

1. Sprinkle chops with all-purpose seasoning and garlic salt; set aside.

2. In a 5-quart slow cooker, combine corn, green beans, okra, onion, and bell pepper. Place chops on top of vegetables.

3. In a medium bowl, stir together chicken broth and gravy mix. Pour over chops.

4. Cover and cook on LOW heat setting for 5 to 7 hours.

5. Serve with thyme (optional).

Southwestern Smothered Chops

Prep 10 minutes
Cook LOW 5 to 7 hours
Makes 4 servings

4   center-cut pork chops, cut 1 inch thick
2   teaspoons Mexican seasoning, *McCormick*®
1   can (15-ounce) low-sodium black beans, rinsed and drained, *S&W*®
1   package (10-ounce) frozen whole-kernel corn, *Birds Eye*®
½   cup frozen chopped onion, *Ore-Ida*®
1   can (10-ounce) condensed creamy chicken verde soup, *Campbell's*®
¾   cup salsa with cilantro, *Pace*®
     Fresh cilantro sprigs (optional)

1. Sprinkle chops with Mexican seasoning; set aside.

2. In a 5-quart slow cooker, combine beans, corn, and onion. Place chops on top of vegetables.

3. In a medium bowl, stir together soup and salsa. Pour over chops.

4. Cover and cook on LOW heat setting for 5 to 7 hours.

5. Serve with cilantro (optional).

Hawaiian Ham with Pineapple and Snap Peas

Prep 10 minutes
Cook LOW 6 to 8 hours
Makes 6 servings

3	pounds smoked, partially cooked picnic ham
2	cans (20 ounces each) pineapple chunks, *Dole*®
1	bottle (10-ounce) teriyaki sauce, *Kikkoman*®
½	cup packed brown sugar, *C&H*®
2	bags (8 ounces each) washed, stringless sugar snap peas, *Mann's*®
	Hot cooked rice (optional)

1. Place ham in a 5- to 6-quart slow cooker, cutting into smaller pieces if necessary to fit slow cooker. Add undrained pineapple and teriyaki sauce. Sprinkle with brown sugar.

2. Cover and cook on LOW heat setting for 5½ to 7½ hours. Stir in snap peas. Cover and cook for 30 minutes more or until an instant-read thermometer inserted into center of ham not touching bone reaches 160 degrees F.

3. Serve with cooked rice (optional).

Sweet Potato-Sausage Gumbo

Prep 15 minutes
Cook LOW 6 to 8 hours
Makes 6 servings

In New Orleans, gumbo is served with yams. This recipe adds them right to the pot, where their sweetness plays off spicy andouille sausage. To save time, this recipe calls for a gumbo mix instead of making a roux.

3	cans (14 ounces each) reduced-sodium chicken broth, *Swanson*®
1	can (14.5-ounce) diced tomatoes with onion, celery, and bell pepper, *Hunt's*®
1	package (13-ounce) fully cooked andouille sausage, sliced, *Aidells*®
1	large sweet potato, peeled and diced into ½-inch pieces
1	box (7-ounce) gumbo mix with rice, *Zatarain's*®

1. In a 4-quart slow cooker, stir together chicken broth, undrained tomatoes, sausage, sweet potato, and gumbo mix until combined.

2. Cover and cook on LOW heat setting for 6 to 8 hours or until sweet potatoes are cooked through.

Italian Chicken

Prep 10 minutes
Cook LOW 5 to 7 hours
Makes 6 servings

2 pounds boneless, skinless chicken breast halves
1 can (28-ounce) whole peeled tomatoes, drained, *Progresso*®
2 packages (8 ounces each) frozen artichoke hearts, thawed, *C&W*®
1 can (15-ounce) pinto beans, rinsed and drained, *Bush's*®
1 package (8-ounce) presliced fresh mushrooms
1 box (1.4-ounce) vegetable soup mix, *Knorr*®
1 can (10.75-ounce) condensed cream of chicken soup, *Campbell's*®
1/3 cup Italian salad dressing, *Newman's Own*®
Hot cooked pasta (optional)
Chopped fresh parsley (optional)

1. Trim fat from chicken; set chicken aside.

2. In a 5-quart slow cooker, combine tomatoes, artichoke hearts, beans, mushrooms, and vegetable soup mix. Add chicken.

3. In a small bowl, combine soup and salad dressing. Pour over chicken.

4. Cover and cook on LOW heat setting for 5 to 7 hours.

5. Shred or cut chicken breast halves into bite-size pieces (optional). Serve chicken and vegetables over cooked pasta (optional). Sprinkle with parsley (optional).

Chicken alla Cacciatora

Prep 10 minutes
Cook LOW 6 to 8 hours
Makes 4 servings

1½ pounds boneless, skinless chicken breast halves
1 can (28-ounce) whole peeled tomatoes, *Progresso*®
1 package (8-ounce) presliced fresh mushrooms
1 cup frozen loose-pack sliced carrots, *C&W*®
2 ribs celery, sliced
1 cup condensed cream of chicken soup, *Campbell's*®
1 cup reduced-sodium chicken broth, *Swanson*®
2 teaspoons salt-free chicken seasoning, *McCormick*®
Hot cooked pasta (optional)

1. Trim fat from chicken; set chicken aside.

2. In a 5-quart slow cooker, combine undrained tomatoes, mushrooms, carrots, and celery. Place chicken on top of vegetables.

3. In a medium bowl, stir together soup, chicken broth, and chicken seasoning. Pour over chicken.

4. Cover and cook on LOW heat setting for 6 to 8 hours.

5. Serve with cooked pasta (optional).

Chicken with New Potatoes and Spinach

Prep 15 minutes
Cook LOW 5 to 6 hours
Makes 4 servings

1½	pounds boneless, skinless chicken breast halves
1	teaspoon ground black pepper
½	teaspoon salt
1	pound small red potatoes, quartered
2	bags (6 ounces each) fresh baby spinach, *Ready Pac*®
1	cup frozen chopped onion, *Ore-Ida*®
1	can (10.75-ounce) condensed cream of celery soup, *Campbell's*®

1. Preheat broiler. Line a baking sheet with aluminum foil. Trim fat from chicken. Sprinkle chicken with pepper and salt. Arrange chicken pieces on prepared baking sheet, smooth sides up. Broil 6 inches from heat for 10 minutes or until chicken is golden.*

2. In a 4-quart slow cooker, arrange potato quarters. Top with spinach and onion. Spoon half of the soup on top of vegetables. Add chicken. Spread with remaining soup.

3. Cover and cook on LOW heat setting for 5 to 6 hours.

*Note: This step may be omitted, but it produces a better-flavored dish.

Moroccan Chicken with Couscous

Prep 15 minutes
Cook LOW 5 to 7 hours Stand 5 minutes
Makes 6 servings

1	teaspoon ground cinnamon, *McCormick*®
1	teaspoon ground coriander, *McCormick*®
1	teaspoon ground black pepper
½	teaspoon salt
2	pounds boneless, skinless chicken breast halves
1	cup frozen loose-pack sliced carrots, *C&W*®
1	onion, cut into 8 wedges through core
2	ribs celery, sliced
⅓	cup orange-flavor dried plums (prunes), *Sunsweet*®
⅓	cup dried apricots, *Sun-Maid*®
1½	cups reduced-sodium chicken broth, *Swanson*®
1	box (10-ounce) instant couscous, *Near East*®

1. In a small bowl, combine cinnamon, coriander, pepper, and salt; set aside. Remove fat from chicken. Sprinkle both sides of chicken with seasoning mixture; set aside.

2. In a 5-quart slow cooker, combine carrots, onion, celery, dried plums, and apricots. Add chicken. Pour chicken broth over chicken.

3. Cover and cook on LOW heat setting for 5 to 7 hours. Using a slotted spoon, transfer chicken, vegetables, and fruit to a serving platter. Tent with aluminum foil to keep warm.

4. Transfer 2 cups of broth mixture from slow cooker to a saucepan. Bring to a boil. Stir in couscous; remove from heat. Cover; let stand for 5 minutes. Fluff couscous with a fork. Serve couscous with chicken, vegetables, and fruit.

Five-Ingredient Dishes

I love cooking from scratch. I love planning the perfect menu, shopping for the freshest ingredients, and creating a beautiful meal for my family and friends. And if I did all of the former, I would have scarce time left for the latter. Five ingredients is doable for everybody, from working professionals to on-the-go soccer moms. Paring down ingredients doesn't mean skimping on taste. The trick to streamlining is to "beef up" recipes with culinary overachievers—big-flavor foods that deliver maximum zip with minimal ingredients. Tangy BBQ sauce mixes with cranberry jelly to perk up pulled pork; garlic and herbs give game hens a kick; Italian seasoning and spiced tomatoes make bread soup sing. If you're looking for quick cooking, take five—then sit back and enjoy the meal.

The Recipes

Slow-Simmered
Chipotle Rib Sandwiches

Prep 20 minutes
Cook LOW 10 to 12 hours
Makes 6 servings

1	onion, sliced
3½	pounds beef short ribs
1	envelope (1.1-ounce) beef onion soup mix, *Lipton*®
1	jar (16-ounce) chipotle salsa, *Pace*®
½	cup ale-style beer
	Kaiser rolls, split and toasted (optional)

1. Place onion in a 4- to 5-quart slow cooker. Add ribs to slow cooker, meaty sides up. Sprinkle with onion soup mix. Add salsa and beer.

2. Cover and cook on LOW heat setting for 10 to 12 hours.

3. Transfer ribs from slow cooker to a cutting board. Tent with aluminum foil until cool enough to handle. Using tongs, transfer onions from cooking juices to a serving bowl. Remove meat from bones (it should fall off); shred. Serve on kaiser rolls (optional). Serve with onions and cooking juices.

Cuban-Style Flank Steak

Prep 10 minutes
Cook LOW 6 to 8 hours
Makes 6 servings

1	jar (16-ounce) lime and garlic salsa, *Pace*®
2½	pounds beef flank steak
2	cans (15 ounces each) Caribbean black beans, rinsed and drained, *S&W*®
1	cup frozen chopped onion, *Ore-Ida*®
3	tablespoons frozen orange juice concentrate, thawed, *Minute Maid*®
	Hot cooked rice (optional)
	Fresh cilantro sprigs (optional)
	Lime wedges (optional)

1. Using a wire mesh strainer set over a small bowl, drain liquid from salsa; set salsa aside. Discard liquid.

2. Cut steak across the grain into 5- to 6-inch strips; set aside.

3. In a 4- to 5-quart slow cooker, stir together beans, onion, and orange juice concentrate until thoroughly combined. Add steak strips and cover with salsa.

4. Cover and cook on LOW heat setting for 6 to 8 hours. Serve with cooked rice, cilantro, and lime wedges (optional).

Sweet-and-Sour Beef

Prep 15 minutes
Cook LOW 8 to 10 hours
Makes 6 servings

3	pounds beef chuck roast
	Salt and ground black pepper
2	red bell peppers, cut into strips
1	cup chili sauce,* *Heinz*®
½	cup frozen chopped onion, *Ore-Ida*®
1	packet (0.75-ounce) sweet-and-sour seasoning mix, *Sun-Bird*®
	Hot steamed rice (optional)
	Scallions (green onions), slivered (optional)

1. Sprinkle roast with salt and black pepper; cut into 1½-inch pieces. Place in a 5-quart slow cooker. In a medium bowl, combine bell peppers, chili sauce, onion, and sweet-and-sour seasoning mix. Spoon over roast.

2. Cover and cook on LOW heat setting for 8 to 10 hours.

3. Serve over steamed rice (optional). Top with scallions (optional).

*Note: If you can't find chili sauce near the ketchup in the supermarket, look for it in the Asian food section.

Five-Spice Beef Stew

Prep 10 minutes
Cook LOW 8 to 10 hours
Makes 6 servings

2	pounds beef stew meat, cut into 1-inch pieces
1	pound baby carrots
2	cans (14.5 ounces each) diced tomatoes with onion and garlic, *S&W*®
¾	cup reduced-sodium beef broth, *Swanson*®
1	tablespoon five-spice powder, *McCormick*®
	Salt and ground black pepper
	Hot mashed potatoes (optional)

1. In a 4- to 5-quart slow cooker, stir together beef stew meat, carrots, undrained tomatoes, beef broth, and five-spice powder until thoroughly combined.

2. Cover and cook on LOW heat setting for 8 to 10 hours. Season with salt and pepper.

3. Serve with mashed potatoes (optional).

Mom's Best BBQ Brisket

Prep 15 minutes
Cook HIGH 1 hour; plus 8 to 10 hours on LOW
Makes 6 servings

Beef brisket is a tougher cut that becomes more tender the longer you cook it. Sauce it up with jalapeños, BBQ sauce, and onion soup mix and let it moist-marinate all day. Great for sandwiches!

$3\frac{1}{2}$ pounds beef brisket
    Salt and ground black pepper
1 large sweet onion, sliced
1 jalapeño chile pepper, diced*
1 packet (1-ounce) onion soup mix, *Lipton*®
1 bottle (14-ounce) barbecue sauce, *Bull's-Eye*®

1. Trim fat from brisket. Sprinkle brisket with salt and black pepper; set aside.

2. In a 5-quart slow cooker, arrange onion slices. Place brisket on top. Add jalapeño pepper and onion soup mix. Pour barbecue sauce over all.

3. Cover and cook on HIGH heat setting for 1 hour. Turn to LOW heat setting; cook for 8 to 10 hours more.

*Note: Because chile peppers contain volatile oils that can burn your skin and eyes, avoid direct contact with them as much as possible. When working with chile peppers, wear plastic or rubber gloves. If your bare hands do touch the peppers, wash your hands and nails well with soap and warm water.

Orange-Cinnamon Pork Chops

Prep 10 minutes
Cook LOW 4½ to 6 hours
Makes 4 servings

4	center-cut pork chops, cut 1 inch thick
	Salt and ground black pepper
1	cup frozen chopped onion, *Ore-Ida*®
1	jar (16-ounce) orange marmalade, *Knott's Berry Farm*®
¼	cup Chardonnay or other white wine
4	sticks (2 inches each) cinnamon
	Orange slices, halved (optional)

1. Sprinkle chops with salt and pepper; set aside.

2. Place onion in a 4-quart slow cooker. Place chops on top. Spoon marmalade over chops. Pour wine over all. Add cinnamon sticks.

3. Cover and cook on LOW heat setting for 4½ to 6 hours. Discard cinnamon sticks.

4. Serve with orange slices (optional).

Cranberry BBQ Pulled Pork

Prep 10 minutes
Cook LOW 8 to 10 hours
Makes 8 servings

1	3- to 4-pound pork shoulder roast
1	tablespoon Montreal steak seasoning, *McCormick*®
1½	large onions, sliced
1	bottle (18-ounce) hickory-flavor barbecue sauce, *Bull's-Eye*®
2	cans (16 ounces each) whole cranberry sauce, *Ocean Spray*®
	Sandwich rolls or buns, split and toasted (optional)

1. Sprinkle roast with steak seasoning; set aside.

2. In a 5-quart slow cooker, arrange onion slices. Top with roast.

3. In a medium bowl, combine barbecue sauce and cranberry sauce. Pour over roast.

4. Cover and cook on LOW heat setting for 8 to 10 hours.

5. Transfer roast from slow cooker to a cutting board. Tent with aluminum foil until cool enough to handle. Using tongs, transfer onions to a serving bowl. Pull or shred roast into bite-size pieces.

6. Using a wire mesh strainer, strain cooking juices into a medium bowl. Serve meat on sandwich rolls (optional). Serve with onions and cooking juices.

Moo Shu Pork

Prep 15 minutes
Cook HIGH $1\frac{1}{2}$ hours plus $1\frac{1}{2}$ hours
Makes 6 servings

$1\frac{1}{2}$	**pounds boneless thinly cut pork loin chops**
	Salt and ground black pepper
2	**bottles (8.5 ounces each) hoisin sauce, _Lee Kum Kee_®**
3	**tablespoons soy sauce, _Kikkoman_®**
4	**scallions (green onions), chopped**
2	**bags (16 ounces each) cole slaw mix, _Fresh Express_®**
	Warmed taco-size flour tortillas or hot cooked rice (optional)

1. Sprinkle chops with salt and pepper; cut into thin bite-size strips.

2. In a 5-quart slow cooker, stir together pork strips, hoisin sauce, and soy sauce until thoroughly combined.

3. Cover and cook on HIGH heat setting for $1\frac{1}{2}$ hours. Refrigerate 2 tablespoons of the scallions. Stir the remaining scallions and cole slaw mix into slow cooker until well combined. Cover and cook for another $1\frac{1}{2}$ hours.

4. Serve in warmed tortillas or over cooked rice (optional). Sprinkle with reserved 2 tablespoons scallions.

Creamy Chicken with Artichokes and Mushrooms

Prep 10 minutes
Cook LOW 4 to 6 hours
Makes 6 servings

2   packages (8 ounces each) frozen artichoke hearts, *C&W*®
1   package (8-ounce) presliced fresh mushrooms
2   pounds boneless, skinless chicken breast halves, cut into
     1-inch cubes
2   cans (10.75 ounces each) condensed cream of chicken
     soup, *Campbell's*®
1   packet (0.87-ounce) tomato, garlic, and basil marinade seasoning
     mix, *McCormick*®
     Hot cooked dried mostaccioli, *Barilla*® (optional)

1. In a 5-quart slow cooker, combine artichokes and mushrooms. Place chicken on top of vegetables.

2. In a medium bowl, combine soup and marinade seasoning mix. Pour over chicken.

3. Cover and cook on LOW heat setting for 4 to 6 hours.

4. Serve over cooked mostaccioli (optional).

Southern Smothered Chicken

Prep 15 minutes
Cook LOW 4 to 6 hours
Makes 6 servings

Smothered chicken is sacred in the South. This genteel version calls for chicken breasts instead of frying chicken, simmered with baby corn, mushrooms, and onions and served with a mound of mashed potatoes.

5   boneless, skinless chicken breast halves (about 1½ pounds total)
1   package (8-ounce) presliced fresh mushrooms
1   can (16-ounce) baby corn, drained, *Reese*®
1   large onion, cut into ¼-inch-thick slices
2   cans (10.75 ounces each) condensed creamy chicken verde soup, *Campbell's*®
    Fresh thyme (optional)
    Cracked black pepper (optional)

1. Trim fat from chicken; set chicken aside.

2. In a 5-quart slow cooker, combine mushrooms, corn, and onion. Place chicken on top of vegetables. Spoon soup over all.

3. Cover and cook on LOW heat setting for 4 to 6 hours.

4. Serve with thyme sprigs and cracked pepper (optional).

Mango Barbecued Chicken

Prep 15 minutes
Cook HIGH 4 to 6 hours
Makes 6 servings

6   boneless, skinless chicken breast halves (about 2 pounds total)
    Salt and ground black pepper
1   onion, thickly sliced
1   bag (16-ounce) frozen mango chunks, *Dole*®
1   bottle (18-ounce) spicy honey-flavor barbecue sauce, *Kraft*®
¼   cup dark rum, *Myers's*®

1. Remove fat from chicken. Sprinkle chicken with salt and pepper; set aside.

2. In a 4- to 5-quart slow cooker, arrange onion slices. Add chicken and mango chunks. In a medium bowl, combine barbecue sauce and rum. Pour over chicken and mango chunks. Cover and cook on HIGH heat setting for 4 to 6 hours.

3. Transfer chicken to a serving bowl. Cover with aluminum foil to keep warm. Carefully transfer cooking juices to a blender. Cover; place a kitchen towel on top of lid. Blend just until mixture is combined. Serve with chicken.

Garlic Game Hens

Prep 25 minutes
Cook HIGH 3 to 5 hours
Makes 8 servings

4	Cornish game hens
	Extra-virgin olive oil, *Bertolli*® (optional)
	Salt and ground black pepper (optional)
1	can (10.75-ounce) condensed cream of chicken soup, *Campbell's*®
2	tablespoons bottled lemon juice, *ReaLemon*®
1	tablespoon herbes de Provence, *McCormick*®
1	jar (6-ounce, about 40 cloves) prepeeled whole garlic cloves, *Christopher Ranch*®
	Chopped fresh herbs (optional)

1. With kitchen scissors, cut the backbone from each hen. Split the hens in half through the breast bone. Trim off excess skin and fat.

2. Preheat broiler. Line a baking sheet with aluminum foil. Place hen halves on prepared baking sheet and rub each on both sides with olive oil. Sprinkle on both sides with salt and pepper. Turn hen halves skin sides up. Broil 4 to 6 inches from heat for 8 to 10 minutes or until skin is golden and begins to crisp.*

3. In a medium bowl, combine soup, lemon juice, and herbes de Provence; set aside.

4. Place one-third of the garlic in a 5-quart slow cooker. Add 4 of the hen halves, another one-third of the garlic, half of the soup mixture, and the remaining hen halves. Add remaining garlic and soup mixture.

5. Cover and cook on HIGH heat setting for 3 to 5 hours.

6. Serve with chopped herbs (optional).

*Note: This step may be omitted, but it produces a better-flavored dish.

Hot and Sticky Wings

Prep 25 minutes
Cook HIGH 2½ to 3½ hours **Cool** 15 minutes
Makes 6 servings

3	pounds chicken wings
1	jar (18-ounce) apricot-pineapple preserves, *Smucker's*®
¼	cup ketchup, *Heinz*®
1	packet (1.25-ounce) chipotle taco seasoning mix, *Ortega*®
1	jalapeño chile pepper, finely diced*
	Blue cheese salad dressing (optional)
	Celery leaves (optional)

1. Preheat broiler. Line a baking sheet with aluminum foil. Remove tips from chicken wings; discard tips, Cut wings into sections. Place wings, skin sides up, on prepared baking sheet. Broil 4 to 6 inches from heat for 8 to 10 minutes or until skin is golden and begins to crisp.**

2. Place wings in a 4-quart slow cooker. In a medium bowl, combine preserves, ketchup, taco seasoning mix, and jalapeño pepper. Pour over wings, stirring to coat.

3. Cover and cook on HIGH heat setting for 2½ to 3½ hours. Cool at least 15 minutes. (This allows cooking juices to thicken.)

4. Serve warm or at room temperature with blue cheese salad dressing and celery leaves (optional).

*Note: Because chile peppers contain volatile oils that can burn your skin and eyes, avoid direct contact with them as much as possible. When working with chile peppers, wear plastic or rubber gloves. If your bare hands do touch the peppers, wash your hands and nails well with soap and warm water.

**Note: This step may be omitted, but it produces a better-flavored dish.

Ziti with Spicy Ragout

Prep 25 minutes
Cook LOW 2 to 4 hours
Makes 6 servings

Exuberant Merlot and a double dose of spicing from Italian sausage and red pepper pasta sauce make a boldly seasoned ragout that's a hearty topping for ziti. Finish with a generous sprinkling of Parmesan.

1   **pound dried ziti pasta**
1¼   **pounds bulk hot Italian sausage**
1   **jar (26-ounce) spicy red pepper pasta sauce, *Classico*®**
2   **cups shredded Italian cheese blend, *Kraft*®**
1   **cup red wine, Merlot**
       Shredded Parmesan cheese, *Kraft*® (optional)

1. In a large pot of salted, boiling water, cook ziti about 10 minutes or just until al dente. Drain and transfer to a 4- to 5-quart slow cooker.

2. In a large skillet, over medium-high heat, cook and stir sausage until browned, breaking up clumps. Transfer to slow cooker. Stir in pasta sauce, Italian cheese blend, and wine.

3. Cover and cook on LOW heat setting for 2 to 4 hours.

4. Serve with shredded Parmesan cheese (optional).

Italian Bread Soup

Prep 10 minutes
Cook HIGH 4 to 6 hours
Makes 4 servings

2   cans (14 ounces each) reduced-sodium chicken broth, *Swanson*®
4   cans (14.5 ounces each) organic fire-roasted diced
     tomatoes, *Muir Glen*®
3   cups Caesar-style croutons
1   cup frozen chopped onion, *Ore-Ida*®
1   packet (0.7-ounce) Italian salad dressing mix, *Good Seasons*®
     Salt and ground black pepper
     Grated Parmesan cheese, *DiGiorno*® (optional)
     Shredded fresh basil (optional)

1. In a 4-quart slow cooker, combine chicken broth, undrained tomatoes, croutons, onion, and salad dressing mix.

2. Cook on HIGH heat setting for 4 to 6 hours. Season with salt and pepper.

3. Serve with Parmesan cheese and basil (optional).

Casseroles

When you hear "casserole," you think family. My friend Hilary grew up with great cooking. She took her mother's recipes off to college and has been quick cooking ever since. Now she's the mom. With two daughters in grade school and husband, AJ, (who looks just like Harry Potter) busy in his own home office, juggling two careers, two kids, and three meals a day is everyday life in the Lentini household. Casseroles make life manageable, helping you serve heartwarming dishes like Tamale Pie and Scalloped Ham and Potatoes, just like Mom used to make. Jazz up the ingredients and feisty Jambalaya Bake and sumptuous Duck and Sausage Cassoulet cook colorfully for company. The question isn't "What's for dinner?" The question is "What did you do today?" Casseroles do the work, so you can spend time with those you care most about.

The Recipes

Chicken Tetrazzini

Prep 25 minutes
Bake 30 minutes
Makes 6 servings

3	tablespoons butter
1	package (8-ounce) presliced fresh mushrooms
1	teaspoon bottled chopped garlic, *Christopher Ranch*®
1	can (14-ounce) reduced-sodium chicken broth, *Swanson*®
1	packet (1.8-ounce) white sauce mix, *Knorr*®
½	cup half-and-half
2	tablespoons sherry, *Christian Brothers*®
1	cup shredded Swiss cheese, *Kraft*®
4	ounces dried spaghetti, broken in half, *Barilla*®
2	cups cooked chicken white meat, cubed
¼	cup grated Parmesan cheese, *DiGiorno*®

1. Preheat oven to 325 degrees F. Lightly butter a 2-quart casserole with some of the butter; set aside.

2. In a large saucepan, over medium heat, melt remaining butter. Add mushrooms and garlic. Cook and stir until mushrooms are soft. Transfer to a medium bowl; set aside.

3. In the same saucepan, whisk together chicken broth and sauce mix. Over high heat, bring to a boil. Add half-and-half and sherry. Stir in Swiss cheese. Cook and stir until cheese is melted.

4. Add pasta to saucepan. Cook over low heat for 8 to 10 minutes or until pasta is al dente, stirring occasionally. Remove from heat. Stir in chicken and mushroom mixture.

5. Transfer to prepared casserole. Sprinkle with Parmesan cheese. Bake in preheated oven for 30 minutes or until heated through.

Creamy Chicken with Broccoli Shells

Prep 30 minutes
Bake 35 minutes plus 5 minutes
Makes 6 servings

1	box (12-ounce) dried jumbo pasta shells, *Barilla*®
1	package (10-ounce) frozen chopped broccoli, *C&W*®
2	tablespoons water
1	large egg
1	container (15-ounce) ricotta cheese, *Precious*®
1	cup cooked chicken, chopped
2	cups shredded mozzarella cheese, *Kraft*®
1	tablespoon dried Italian seasoning, *McCormick*®
1	teaspoon salt
1	teaspoon ground black pepper
1	jar (16-ounce) roasted garlic Alfredo pasta sauce, *Classico*®

1. Preheat oven to 350 degrees F.

2. In a large pot of salted, boiling water, cook pasta for 12 minutes or just until al dente. Drain and rinse with cold water to stop cooking; drain. Set aside.

3. Place broccoli and the 2 tablespoons water in a microwave-safe bowl. Cover and microwave on high setting (100% power) for 5 minutes. Drain and transfer to a large bowl.

4. In a small bowl, beat egg with a fork. Stir egg, ricotta cheese, chicken, 1 cup of the mozzarella cheese, Italian seasoning, salt, and pepper into broccoli until thoroughly combined.

5. Spoon 1 cup of the pasta sauce into a 13×9-inch baking dish; set aside. Fill 21 to 24 pasta shells with chicken mixture. Arrange in baking dish.

6. Spoon remaining pasta sauce over shells. Sprinkle with remaining mozzarella. Cover loosely with aluminum foil.

7. Bake in preheated oven for 35 to 40 minutes. Remove aluminum foil and cook for 5 to 10 minutes more.

Jambalaya Bake

Prep 15 minutes
Bake 70 minutes
Makes 6 servings

1 **pound boneless, skinless chicken breast halves, cut into 1-inch pieces**
1 **can (14.5-ounce) diced tomatoes with onion, celery, and bell pepper, *Hunt's*®**
1 **can (14-ounce) reduced-sodium chicken broth, *Swanson*®**
8 **ounces hot Louisiana sausage, cut into 1-inch pieces, *Farmer John*®**
1 **box (8-ounce) jambalaya mix, *Zatarain's*®**

1. Preheat oven to 350 degrees F.

2. In a 2-quart casserole, stir together chicken, undrained tomatoes, chicken broth, sausage, and jambalaya mix until thoroughly combined. Cover tightly with aluminum foil.

3. Bake in preheated oven for 70 to 85 minutes.

Turkey Potpie with Pepper Biscuit Topping

Prep 20 minutes
Bake 1 hour plus 15 minutes
Makes 6 servings

1	pound boneless, skinless turkey breast, cut into bite-size pieces
2	cans (10.75 ounces each) condensed cream of chicken soup, *Campbell's*®
1	large red potato, diced
½	package (16-ounce) frozen loose-pack mixed vegetables (carrots, corn, peas, green beans), thawed, *C&W*®
1	cup frozen chopped onion, *Ore-Ida*®
1	teaspoon salt-free chicken seasoning, *McCormick*®
1	can (16-ounce) refrigerated biscuits, *Pillsbury Grands!*®
1	tablespoon butter, melted
¾	teaspoon ground black pepper

1. Preheat oven to 350 degrees F. Line a baking sheet with aluminum foil; set aside.

2. In a large bowl, stir together turkey, soup, potato, mixed vegetables, onion, and chicken seasoning until thoroughly combined. Transfer to a 2½-quart casserole. Cover with aluminum foil and place on prepared baking sheet.

3. Bake in preheated oven for 1 hour or until hot and bubbling. Remove from oven and discard aluminum foil. Gently stir mixture to evenly distribute heat.

4. Arrange 6 biscuits on top of casserole.* Brush tops of biscuits with melted butter. Sprinkle with pepper. Bake for 15 to 18 minutes more or until biscuits have risen and are golden brown.

*Note: Place the extra biscuits in a pie plate and bake alongside the casserole for 15 to 18 minutes or until biscuits have risen and are golden brown. Serve with casserole or cool on a wire rack to use at another meal.

Turkey Day Casserole

Prep 15 minutes
Bake 30 minutes
Makes 6 servings

Layers of cranberry sauce, stuffing, and mashed potatoes in a puddle of gravy capture the flavor of Thanksgiving year-round. Just skillet-brown the turkey, then put everything else in straight from the package.

1	container (24-ounce) mashed potatoes, *Country Crock®*
1	pound uncooked ground turkey
1	box (6-ounce) stuffing for turkey, *Stove Top®*
1	can (16-ounce) whole cranberry sauce, *Ocean Spray®*
2	jars (12 ounces each) homestyle turkey gravy, *Heinz®*
2	tablespoons butter, cut into small pieces

1. Preheat oven to 350 degrees F. Microwave mashed potatoes, uncovered, in container on high setting (100% power) for 1 minute. Stir to break up potatoes; set aside.

2. In a medium saucepan, over medium heat, cook and stir turkey until browned, breaking up clumps. Drain off fat; set aside.

3. Spread dry stuffing mix in the bottom of a $2\frac{1}{2}$-quart casserole. Top with cranberry sauce. Layer turkey and 1 jar of the gravy. Spread mashed potatoes evenly over layers in casserole. Dot with butter pieces.

4. Bake in preheated oven for 30 to 40 minutes.

5. To serve, heat remaining gravy according to label directions. Serve with casserole.

Tamale Pie

Prep 20 minutes
Bake 45 minutes plus 5 minutes
Makes 4 servings

1	pound ground beef
1	can (10-ounce) diced tomatoes and green chiles, drained, *Ro-Tel*®
1	cup chunky salsa verde, *La Victoria*®
1	package (8.5-ounce) corn muffin mix, *Jiffy*®
1	cup cream-style corn, *C&W*®
1	can (2.25-ounce) sliced black olives, drained, *Early California*®
1	cup shredded Mexican cheese blend, *Kraft*®

1. Preheat oven to 350 degrees F.

2. In a medium saucepan, over medium heat, cook and stir ground beef until browned, breaking up clumps. Drain off fat; stir in tomatoes and salsa until thoroughly combined. Transfer to a 1½-quart casserole.

3. In a small bowl, stir together muffin mix and corn just until combined. Spread over mixture in casserole. Sprinkle with olives.

4. Bake in preheated oven for 45 to 50 minutes or until bubbly. (If edges start to brown, cover with aluminum foil.) Top with cheese. Bake for 5 minutes more or until cheese is melted.

Tex-Mex Turkey Casserole

Prep 15 minutes
Bake 30 minutes
Makes 6 servings

1¼ pounds uncooked ground turkey
1 packet (1.25-ounce) Tex-Mex chili seasoning mix, *McCormick®*
1 can (15-ounce) low-sodium black beans, rinsed and drained, *S&W®*
1 can (11-ounce) mexicorn, *Green Giant®*
1 can (10.75-ounce) condensed creamy ranchero tomato soup, *Campbell's®*
1 can (4-ounce) diced green chile peppers, drained, *La Victoria®*
1 cup crushed tortilla chips, *Tostitos®*
1 cup shredded Mexican cheese blend, *Kraft®*
⅓ cup sliced black olives, drained, *Early California®*
⅓ cup jalapeño chile pepper slices, drained, *Ortega®*
  Sour cream, *Knudsen®* (optional)
  Salsa (optional)

1. Preheat oven to 350 degrees F.

2. In a large skillet, over medium-high heat, cook and stir turkey with chili seasoning mix until turkey is browned, breaking up clumps. Drain off fat; stir in beans, mexicorn, soup, and green chile peppers. Divide mixture among six 8-ounce casseroles.*

3. Cover with crushed tortilla chips and cheese. Sprinkle with olives and jalapeño pepper slices.

4. Bake in preheated oven about 30 minutes or until hot.

5. Serve with sour cream and salsa (optional).

*Note: If you don't have individual casseroles, spoon the mixture into a 2-quart casserole. Cover with crushed tortilla chips and cheese. Sprinkle with olives and jalapeño pepper slices. Bake in preheated oven for 45 to 50 minutes or until hot. Serve as above.

Moussaka

Prep 30 minutes
Bake 1¼ hours
Makes 6 servings

2 russet potatoes, cut into ¼-inch-thick slices
1 pound ground lamb
2 tablespoons Greek seasoning, *Spice Islands*®
1 can (14.5-ounce) diced tomatoes with basil and garlic, *Muir Glen*®
   Extra-virgin olive oil, *Bertolli*®
1 large eggplant, diced (do not peel)
⅓ cup Italian-style bread crumbs, *Progresso*®
⅓ cup grated Parmesan cheese, *DiGiorno*®
2 cans (10.75 ounces each) condensed cream of potato
   soup, *Campbell's*®

1. Preheat oven to 350 degrees F. In a medium pot of boiling water, cook potato slices about 10 minutes or until almost tender; drain well. Set aside.

2. In a large skillet, cook and stir ground lamb with Greek seasoning until meat is browned, breaking up clumps. Drain off fat. Stir in undrained tomatoes; set aside.

3. In another large skillet, heat 2 tablespoons of the olive oil over medium-high heat. Add eggplant; cook and stir for 4 to 5 minutes or until pieces start to soften. Remove from heat; set aside.

4. In a small bowl, combine bread crumbs, Parmesan cheese, and 1 tablespoon of the olive oil; set aside.

5. Coat the sides and bottom of a 2½-quart casserole with olive oil. Layer one-third of the meat mixture, one-third of the eggplant, and one-third of the potatoes. Repeat layers twice more.

6. Top with soup. Sprinkle with bread crumb mixture. Bake in preheated oven for 1¼ to 1½ hours or until potatoes are tender.

Scalloped Ham and Potatoes

Prep 10 minutes
Bake 1 hour
Makes 6 servings

1½	pounds frozen shredded potatoes, *Ore-Ida*®
½	pound diced ham, *Farmland*®
1	cup frozen chopped onion, *Ore-Ida*®
1	package (8-ounce) crumbled sharp cheddar cheese, *Kraft*®
2	cans (10.75 ounces each) condensed cream of mushroom soup, *Campbell's*®
1	cup heavy cream
½	cup grated Parmesan cheese, *DiGiorno*®

1. Preheat oven to 350 degrees F.

2. In a 2½- to 3-quart casserole dish, layer half of the potatoes, half of the ham, half of the onion, and half of the cheese. Spread 1 can of soup evenly over layers. Repeat layers once more. Top with remaining can of soup.

3. Pour cream over layers, tipping the casserole back and forth to allow cream to soak in. Sprinkle with Parmesan cheese.

4. Bake in preheated oven for 1 hour or until heated through.

Sweet Potato Shepherd's Pie

Prep 15 minutes
Bake 45 minutes
Makes 6 servings

1	container (23-ounce) mashed sweet potatoes, *Country Crock*®
1½	pounds pork tenderloin, cut into 1-inch pieces
	Salt and ground black pepper
1	package (16-ounce) frozen petite mixed vegetables, *C&W*®
1	can (10.75-ounce) condensed cream of mushroom soup with roasted garlic, *Campbell's*®
2	teaspoons salt-free garlic-and-herb seasoning, *McCormick*®

1. Preheat oven to 350 degrees F. Microwave sweet potatoes, uncovered, in container on high setting (100% power) for 2 minutes. Stir to break up potatoes; set aside. Sprinkle pork with salt and pepper.

2. In a 2½-quart casserole, stir together pork, vegetables, soup, and garlic-and-herb seasoning until thoroughly combined. Spread sweet potatoes evenly over pork mixture.*

3. Bake in preheated oven for 45 to 55 minutes or until bubbly.

*Note: For a fancier presentation, use a pastry bag and tip to pipe the sweet potatoes in a lattice design on top of the pork mixture. Or spoon the sweet potatoes into a plastic bag, snip off one corner, and pipe the potatoes on top of the pork mixture.

Sausage Florentine

Prep 30 minutes
Bake 45 minutes
Makes 6 servings

8	ounces dried mini penne pasta, *Barilla*®
2	packages (12 ounces each) frozen spinach soufflé, *Stouffer's*®
1	pound sweet Italian sausage links, sliced
1	package (8-ounce) presliced fresh mushrooms
1½	cups half-and-half
1	can (10.75-ounce) condensed cream of celery soup, *Campbell's*®
1	carton (8-ounce) sour cream, *Knudsen*®
	Diced fresh tomatoes (optional)

1. Preheat oven to 350 degrees F. In a large pot of salted, boiling water, cook pasta according to package directions; drain. Transfer to a large bowl; set aside. Microwave both packages of spinach soufflé on high setting (100% power) for 10 minutes (half of total cooking time); set aside.

2. In a large skillet, over medium heat, cook and stir sausage until cooked through. Drain off fat. Stir into cooked pasta. Stir mushrooms, half-and-half, soup, and sour cream into pasta mixture until thoroughly combined. Transfer to a 3½- to 4-quart casserole.

3. In a small bowl, stir together both packages of partially cooked spinach soufflé. Spread evenly on top of pasta mixture.

4. Bake in preheated oven for 45 to 55 minutes or until baked through and a knife inserted into spinach soufflé comes out clean.

5. Sprinkle with tomatoes (optional).

Polenta Lasagna Puttanesca

Prep 25 minutes
Bake 30 minutes plus 30 minutes
Makes 8 servings

"Easy" is a double entendre with this dish since "puttanesca" in Italian implies "easy virtue." It lives up to its colorful heritage with a spirited tomato-sausage sauce over polenta, a cornmeal mush, instead of noodles.

$1\frac{1}{2}$	pounds bulk hot Italian sausage
$\frac{1}{3}$	cup sliced black olives, drained, *Early California*®
$\frac{1}{3}$	cup pimiento-stuffed green olives, sliced, *Star*®
1	jar (26-ounce) roasted garlic pasta sauce, *Classico*®
1	large egg
1	container (15-ounce) ricotta cheese, *Precious*®
2	tubes (16 ounces each) polenta, cut into $\frac{1}{4}$-inch-thick slices, *Monterey Foods*®
2	cups shredded mozzarella cheese, *Kraft*®
$\frac{1}{2}$	cup grated Parmesan cheese, *DiGiorno*®

1. Preheat oven to 350 degrees F.

2. In a large skillet, over medium-high heat, cook and stir sausage until browned, breaking up clumps. Drain off fat. Stir in black olives, green olives, and one-third of the pasta sauce; set aside.

3. In a medium bowl, beat egg with a fork. Stir in ricotta cheese until thoroughly combined; set aside.

4. Spread half of the remaining pasta sauce evenly into the bottom of a 13×9-inch baking dish. Layer in half of the sliced polenta. Top with sausage mixture and ricotta cheese mixture. Sprinkle with half of the mozzarella cheese and half of the Parmesan cheese. Add remaining polenta slices. Top with remaining pasta sauce and remaining cheeses. Cover with aluminum foil.

5. Bake in preheated oven for 30 minutes. Remove aluminum foil; bake for 30 minutes more.

Hoppin' John Casserole

Prep 15 minutes
Bake 70 minutes
Makes 6 servings

1	package (13-ounce) fully cooked andouille sausage, cut into 1-inch pieces, *Aidells®*
1	can (15-ounce) black-eyed peas, rinsed and drained, *Progresso®*
1	box (8-ounce) dirty rice mix, *Zatarain's®*
1	cup thick and chunky mild salsa, *Ortega®*
½	cup frozen chopped bell peppers, *Pictsweet®*
1	can (14-ounce) reduced-sodium chicken broth, *Swanson®*

1. Preheat oven to 350 degrees F.

2. In a 2½- to 3-quart casserole, stir together sausage, black-eyed peas, rice mix, salsa, and bell peppers until thoroughly combined. Pour chicken broth over sausage mixture. Cover with aluminum foil.

3. Bake in preheated oven for 70 to 85 minutes.

Duck and Sausage Cassoulet

Prep 30 minutes
Bake 1 hour
Makes 6 servings

	Canola oil cooking spray, *Mazola® Pure*
1¾	pounds Muscovy duck breast half
	Salt and ground black pepper
2	cans (15 ounces each) Great Northern beans, rinsed and drained, *Bush's®*
1	can (14.5-ounce) diced tomatoes with garlic, basil, and oregano, *Hunt's®*
8	ounces fully cooked kielbasa sausage, sliced
½	cup frozen chopped onion, *Ore-Ida®*
¼	cup real bacon pieces, *Hormel®*
2	teaspoons poultry seasoning, *McCormick®*
1	teaspoon bottled crushed garlic, *Christopher Ranch®*
⅓	cup Italian-style bread crumbs, *Progresso®*

1. Preheat oven to 350 degrees F. Lightly coat a 2½- to 3-quart casserole with cooking spray; set aside. Lightly sprinkle duck on both sides with salt and pepper.

2. Heat a large skillet over medium-high heat. Place duck in skillet, skin side down; cook for 12 to 15 minutes to render fat and crisp skin. Turn; cook for 5 to 6 minutes more or until slightly pink (medium rare). Transfer to a cutting board; set aside.

3. In a large bowl, combine beans, undrained tomatoes, sausage, onion, bacon, poultry seasoning, and garlic.

4. Slice duck breast in half lengthwise, removing skin, if desired. Cut each half into ¼-inch slices. Stir slices into bean mixture until thoroughly combined.

5. Transfer to prepared casserole. Sprinkle with bread crumbs. Bake in preheated oven for 1 hour.

Mediterranean Vegetable Potpie

Prep 15 minutes
Bake 35 minutes
Makes 6 main-dish servings

	Canola oil cooking spray, *Mazola® Pure*
1	package (16-ounce) frozen Mediterranean-style vegetables, thawed, *C&W®*
1	can (15-ounce) garbanzo beans, rinsed and drained, *Bush's®*
1	can (14.5-ounce) diced tomatoes with basil and garlic, *Muir Glen®*
1	can (10.75-ounce) condensed cream of mushroom soup with roasted garlic, *Campbell's®*
1	package (8-ounce) frozen artichoke hearts, thawed, *C&W®*
1	can (4-ounce) sliced olives, drained, *Early California®*
1	can (2.8-ounce) french fried onions, *French's®*
2	teaspoons salt-free garlic herbs, *McCormick®*
7	sheets frozen phyllo dough, thawed, *Athens®*
2	tablespoons butter, melted

1. Preheat oven to 350 degrees F. Lightly coat a 2½-quart rectangular baking dish with cooking spray; set aside.

2. In a large bowl, stir together Mediterranean-style vegetables, beans, undrained tomatoes, soup, artichoke hearts, olives, french fried onions, and garlic herbs until thoroughly combined. Transfer to prepared casserole dish; set aside.

3. Lightly brush each sheet of phyllo dough with butter and stack together. Using kitchen scissors, trim sheets until they are slightly larger than the baking dish. Place phyllo over vegetable mixture and gently press into baking dish, trimming excess to fit dish.

4. Bake in preheated oven for 35 to 40 minutes or until cooked through and phyllo is golden brown. Serve as a vegetarian main dish or as a side dish.

Pasta, Rice & Risotto

As a child, I thought spaghetti was the pinnacle of fine dining. While the noodles bubbled merrily in one pot, I breathed in the heavenly aroma of warm, cheesy tomato sauce from the other. Slow cooking pasta offers the same pleasure in one pot. Penne, ravioli, ziti, even gnocchi—this chapter has them all, lavished with a rainbow of sauces, from reds, whites, and greens to the palest of pinks. Pasta is all-season food, light and summery with a simple tomato sauce or warming in winter sauced with robust meats and creams. There's Golden Mushroom Risotto, suave and sophisticated with a bottle of wine, or Beefy Mac, culinary perfection to a pint-size palate. Gnocchi with Mushroom Sauce is the vegetarian version of nirvana. Pair them with a mixed green salad and crusty bread to soak up the sauce. Superb!

The Recipes

Beefy Mac

Prep 20 minutes
Cook LOW 2 to 4 hours
Makes 6 servings

12	ounces dried elbow macaroni, *Barilla*®
1½	pounds lean ground beef
1	packet (1.5-ounce) beef stew seasoning mix, *Lawry's*®
2	cups shredded four-cheese blend, *Kraft*®
1	can (10.75-ounce) condensed cheddar cheese soup, *Campbell's*®
1	cup frozen chopped onion, *Ore-Ida*®
½	cup reduced-sodium beef broth, *Swanson*®
	Chopped fresh tomato (optional)
	Chopped fresh parsley (optional)

1. In a pot of salted, boiling water, cook macaroni for 5 to 6 minutes or until almost al dente. Drain and transfer to a 5-quart slow cooker.

2. In a large skillet, cook and stir ground beef and beef stew seasoning mix until beef is browned, breaking up clumps. Drain off fat. Stir beef, cheese, soup, onion, and beef broth into pasta in slow cooker.

3. Cover and cook on LOW heat setting for 2 to 4 hours.

4. Serve with chopped tomato and parsley (optional).

Meatball Lasagna

Prep 15 minutes
Cook LOW 3 to 4 hours
Makes 8 servings

2	pounds frozen fully cooked meatballs, thawed, *Armanino*®
1	large egg
1	container (15-ounce) ricotta cheese, *Precious*®
1	tablespoon dried Italian seasoning, *McCormick*®
	Olive oil cooking spray, *Mazola*® *Pure*
2	jars (26 ounces each) roasted garlic pasta sauce, *Classico*®
1	box (9-ounce) no-boil lasagna sheets, *Barilla*®
1	pound thinly sliced provolone cheese

1. Slice meatballs in half; set aside. In a medium bowl, beat egg with a fork. Stir in ricotta cheese and Italian seasoning until combined; set aside.

2. Coat a 5-quart slow cooker with cooking spray. Add ½ cup of the pasta sauce to slow cooker. Add a layer of lasagna noodles, breaking them to fit. Layer with one-third of the meatballs, one-third of the ricotta cheese mixture, and one-third of the provolone cheese. Add 1½ cups of the pasta sauce. Repeat layers twice more. End with noodles and remaining pasta sauce.

3. Cover and cook on LOW heat setting for 3 to 4 hours.

Potted Lasagna

Prep 35 minutes
Cook LOW 3½ to 4½ hours **Stand** 10 minutes
Makes 8 servings

Healthy shredded spinach and pan-browned turkey swimming in an explosive, garlic-rich pesto sauce make potted lasagna cozy food for a cold night. Garnish with grated cheese or garlic bread crumbs.

1	package (10-ounce) frozen chopped spinach, *C&W*®
1	pound uncooked ground turkey
1	jar (10-ounce) pesto sauce, *Classico*®
1	cup frozen chopped onion, *Ore-Ida*®
1	large egg
1	container (15-ounce) ricotta cheese, *Precious*®
1	cup grated Parmesan cheese, *DiGiorno*®
	Canola oil cooking spray, *Mazola*® *Pure*
2	jars (16 ounces each) four-cheese Alfredo pasta sauce, *Classico*®
1	box (9-ounce) no-boil lasagna sheets, *Barilla*®
1	package (16-ounce) shredded mozzarella cheese, *Kraft*®

1. Place spinach in a microwave-safe bowl. Cover and microwave on high setting (100% power) for 6 to 8 minutes. Drain. Let stand until cool enough to handle; squeeze out excess liquid.

2. In a large skillet, over medium-high heat, cook and stir turkey until browned, breaking up clumps. Drain off fat. Stir in pesto sauce and onion; set aside.

3. In a medium bowl, beat egg with a fork. Stir in ricotta cheese, Parmesan cheese, and spinach until combined; set aside.

4. Coat a 5-quart slow cooker with cooking spray. Spoon ¾ cup of the pasta sauce into slow cooker. Top with a layer of lasagna noodles, breaking them to fit. Add ⅓ cup of the ricotta cheese mixture, spreading to edges. Sprinkle one-third of the turkey mixture over the ricotta cheese mixture. Top with 1 cup of the mozzarella cheese. Top with ¾ cup of the pasta sauce. Repeat layers twice more. End with noodles and remaining pasta sauce. Cover and refrigerate remaining mozzarella cheese.

5. Cover slow cooker and cook on LOW heat setting for 3½ to 4½ hours or until noodles are tender.

6. Turn off slow cooker. Sprinkle reserved mozzarella cheese on top of lasagna mixture. Cover; let stand for 10 minutes or until cheese is melted.

Cajun Chicken Pasta

Prep 25 minutes
Cook HIGH 3 to 4 hours
Makes 6 servings

1½   pounds boneless, skinless chicken breast halves,
      cut into bite-size pieces
1   jar (16-ounce) Alfredo pasta sauce, *Classico*®
1   can (14.5-ounce) diced tomatoes with onion, celery, and bell
      pepper, *Hunt's*®
1   can (14-ounce) reduced-sodium chicken broth, *Swanson*®
1   medium red bell pepper, cut into strips
4   teaspoons Cajun seasoning, *McCormick*®
1   pound dried bow tie pasta, *Anthony's*®
      Chopped fresh chives (optional)

1. In a 4-quart slow cooker, stir together chicken, pasta sauce, undrained tomatoes, chicken broth, bell pepper, and Cajun seasoning until thoroughly combined.

2. Cover and cook on HIGH heat setting for 3 to 4 hours.

3. In a large pot of salted, boiling water, cook pasta for 9 to 10 minutes or until al dente. Drain. Serve chicken mixture over pasta. Sprinkle with chives (optional).

Gnocchi with Mushroom Sauce

Prep 20 minutes
Cook LOW 2 to 3 hours
Makes 4 servings

1	package (16-ounce) potato gnocchi, *Alessi®*
2	cans (10.75 ounces each) condensed cream of mushroom soup with roasted garlic, *Campbell's®*
1	package (8-ounce) presliced fresh brown mushrooms
1	cup frozen chopped onion, *Ore-Ida®*
$\frac{1}{2}$	cup Madeira wine, *Paul Masson®*
2	teaspoons dried Italian seasoning, *McCormick®*
	Shredded Parmesan cheese, *Kraft®*
	Chopped fresh parsley (optional)

1. In a large pot of salted, boiling water, cook gnocchi for 3 to 4 minutes. As gnocchi float to top, remove with slotted spoon. Transfer to a 4-quart slow cooker.

2. Stir soup, mushrooms, onion, wine, and Italian seasoning into slow cooker until thoroughly combined.

3. Cover and cook on LOW heat setting for 2 to 3 hours or until heated through.

4. Serve with Parmesan cheese and chopped parsley (optional).

Layered Lamb and Penne

Prep 25 minutes
Cook LOW 3 to 4 hours
Makes 6 servings

12	ounces dried penne pasta, *Barilla®*
1½	pounds ground lamb
1	tablespoon Greek seasoning, *Spice Islands®*
1	can (14.5-ounce) diced tomatoes with basil and garlic, *Muir Glen®*
1	cup frozen chopped onion, *Ore-Ida®*
1	can (3.8-ounce) sliced black olives, drained, *Early California®*
½	cup chopped fresh parsley
1	teaspoon bottled crushed garlic, *Christopher Ranch®*
	Olive oil cooking spray, *Mazola® Pure*
1	pack (4-ounce) crumbled feta cheese, *Saladena®*
2	cans (10.5 ounces each) white sauce, *Aunt Penny's®*

1. In a large pot of salted, boiling water, cook pasta for 7 to 8 minutes or until almost al dente. Drain; set aside.

2. In a large skillet, over high heat, cook and stir lamb with Greek seasoning until lamb is browned, breaking up clumps. Drain off fat. Stir in undrained tomatoes, onion, olives, parsley, and garlic; set aside.

3. Coat a 5-quart slow cooker with cooking spray. Layer half of the lamb mixture, half of the crumbled feta cheese, half of the pasta, and 1 can of the white sauce. Repeat layers.

4. Cover and cook on LOW heat setting for 3 to 4 hours.

Green Chile Risotto with Chicken

Prep 10 minutes
Cook HIGH 2 hours
Makes 6 servings

2   cans (14 ounces each) reduced-sodium chicken broth, *Swanson®*
2   cups converted long-grain rice, *Uncle Ben's®*
1   can (10.75-ounce) condensed creamy chicken verde soup, *Campbell's®*
1   cup frozen chopped onion, *Ore-Ida®*
1   can (4-ounce) diced green chile peppers, *Ortega®*
$\frac{1}{4}$ cup silver tequila
2   tablespoons chopped pimiento, *Dromedary®*
2   packages (6 ounces each) grilled chicken strips, chopped, *Tyson®*
    Shredded pepper Jack cheese
    Finely chopped fresh cilantro (optional)

1. In 5-quart slow cooker, stir together chicken broth, rice, soup, onion, chile peppers, tequila, and pimiento.

2. Cover and cook on HIGH heat setting for 2 hours.

3. Stir in chicken and $\frac{1}{2}$ cup of the cheese. Serve with chopped cilantro and additional cheese (optional).

Pumpkin Risotto with Smoked Turkey

Prep 20 minutes
Cook HIGH 2 hours
Makes 6 servings

2	smoked turkey legs
3	cups Chardonnay or other white wine
2	cups converted long-grain rice, *Uncle Ben's*®
1	can (14-ounce) reduced-sodium chicken broth, *Swanson*®
1	cup canned pumpkin, *Libby's*®
1	teaspoon poultry seasoning, *McCormick*®
¾	teaspoon salt
	Grated Parmesan cheese, *DiGiorno*®
	Salt and ground black pepper
	Fresh sage (optional)

1. Remove skin from turkey legs; remove meat from bones. Discard skin and bones. Chop turkey. Transfer to a 5-quart slow cooker.

2. Stir wine, rice, chicken broth, pumpkin, poultry seasoning, and the ¾ teaspoon salt into slow cooker until thoroughly combined.

3. Cover and cook on HIGH heat setting for 2 hours.

4. Stir in ½ cup of the Parmesan cheese. Season with additional salt and pepper.

5. Serve with sage leaves and additional Parmesan cheese (optional).

Red Wine Risotto

Prep 10 minutes
Cook HIGH 2 hours
Makes 6 servings

1¼   cups **Arborio rice**
1   cup **frozen chopped onion, *Ore-Ida*®**
3   tablespoons **extra-virgin olive oil, *Bertolli*®**
3   cups **reduced-sodium chicken broth, *Swanson*®**
1   cup **Cabernet Sauvignon or other red wine**
      Shredded Parmesan cheese, *Kraft*®
      Chopped fresh basil (optional)

1. In a 4-quart slow cooker, stir together rice, onion, and olive oil until thoroughly combined, making sure rice is well coated. Stir in chicken broth and wine.

2. Cover and cook on HIGH heat setting for 2 hours. (Rice should be slightly wet.)

3. Stir in ½ cup of the Parmesan cheese. Sprinkle with basil and additional Parmesan cheese (optional).

Risotto Carbonara

Prep 10 minutes
Cook HIGH 2 hours
Makes 6 servings

If you're only going to be gone a few hours, a quick risotto is just what you need. This upmarket variation of Pasta Carbonara is a heady mix of chewy and creamy, made densely flavorful with smoky bacon and Parmesan cheese.

3   cups **reduced-sodium chicken broth, *Swanson*®**
2   cups **converted long-grain rice, *Uncle Ben's*®**
2   cups **Chardonnay or other white wine**
1   can (10.5-ounce) **white sauce, *Aunt Penny's*®**
1   cup **frozen chopped onion, *Ore-Ida*®**
1   cup **frozen loose-pack petite peas, *C&W*®**
4   strips **precooked bacon, chopped, *Hormel*®**
      Grated Parmesan cheese, *DiGiorno*®

1. In a 4-quart slow cooker, stir together chicken broth, rice, wine, white sauce, onion, peas, and bacon until thoroughly combined.

2. Cover and cook on HIGH heat setting for 2 hours. (Rice should be slightly wet.)

3. Stir in ⅓ cup of the Parmesan cheese. Serve with additional Parmesan cheese (optional).

Golden Mushroom Risotto

Prep 20 minutes
Cook HIGH 2 hours
Makes 6 servings

1	package (0.5-ounce) dried chanterelle mushrooms*
	Boiling water
2	cans (14 ounces each) reduced-sodium beef broth, *Swanson*®
2	cups converted long-grain rice, *Uncle Ben's*®
1	can (10.75-ounce) condensed golden mushroom soup, *Campbell's*®
1	package (8-ounce) presliced fresh white mushrooms
1	package (6-ounce) presliced portobello mushrooms
1	package (6-ounce) baby bella mushrooms
1	cup frozen chopped onion, *Ore-Ida*®
$\frac{1}{4}$	cup cognac
$\frac{1}{4}$	cup heavy cream
	Shredded Parmesan cheese, *Kraft*®

1. In a medium bowl, combine chanterelle mushrooms with enough boiling water to cover; let stand for 5 minutes. Drain. Transfer to a 5-quart slow cooker.

2. Stir beef broth, rice, soup, white mushrooms, portobello mushrooms, baby bella mushrooms, onion, and cognac into slow cooker until thoroughly combined.

3. Cover and cook on HIGH heat setting for 2 hours.

4. Stir in cream and $\frac{1}{4}$ cup of the Parmesan cheese. Serve with additional Parmesan cheese (optional).

*Note: You may use any variety of wild mushrooms.

Risotto with Blue Cheese, Figs, and Arugula

Prep 10 minutes
Cook HIGH 2 hours
Makes 6 servings

1½   cups Arborio rice
1   cup frozen chopped onion, *Ore-Ida*®
3   tablespoons extra-virgin olive oil, *Bertolli*®
2½   cups chicken broth with roasted garlic, *Swanson*®
½   cup Chardonnay or other white wine
4   ounces prewashed baby arugula
1   cup chopped dried figs, *Mariani*®
      Blue cheese crumbles, *Treasure Cave*®
¼   cup heavy cream (optional)
      Salt and ground black pepper

1. In a 4- to 5-quart slow cooker, stir together rice, onion, and olive oil until thoroughly combined, making sure rice is well coated. Add chicken broth and wine.

2. Cover and cook on HIGH heat setting for 2 hours. Stir in arugula until wilted.

3. Fold in figs and ¾ cup of the blue cheese. Add cream, if needed, to make desired consistency. Season with salt and pepper.

4. Serve with additional blue cheese (optional).

Easiest-Ever Paella

Prep 15 minutes
Cook HIGH 2 hours plus 20 minutes
Makes 6 servings

8	ounces boneless, skinless chicken breast halves, cut into 1-inch pieces
8	ounces fully cooked andouille sausage, cut into 1-inch pieces, *Aidells®*
2	cans (14 ounces each) reduced-sodium chicken broth, *Swanson®*
1	can (14.5-ounce) no-salt-added diced tomatoes, *S&W®*
2	packages (5.6 ounces each) Spanish rice mix, *Lipton®*
1	cup frozen loose-pack petite peas, *C&W®*
½	cup frozen chopped onion, *Ore-Ida®*
1	cup frozen cooked shrimp, thawed

1. In a 4-quart slow cooker, stir together chicken, sausage, chicken broth, undrained tomatoes, Spanish rice mix, peas, and onion until thoroughly combined.

2. Cover and cook on HIGH heat setting for 2 hours. Stir in shrimp. Cover; cook for 20 to 30 minutes or until shrimp is heated through.

Shrimp Pilaf with Peas

Prep 15 minutes
Cook HIGH 2 hours plus 20 minutes
Makes 6 servings

2	cans (10.75 ounces each) condensed shrimp bisque, *Campbell's®*
1	can (14-ounce) vegetable broth, *Swanson®*
2	boxes (6.3 ounces each) garlic-and-herb rice pilaf mix, *Near East®*
2	ribs celery, diced
1	cup frozen chopped onion, *Ore-Ida®*
1	cup frozen loose-pack petite peas, *C&W®*
1	bag (14-ounces) frozen cooked medium shrimp with tails, thawed
	Chopped fresh parsley (optional)
	Lemon wedges (optional)

1. In a 4-quart slow cooker, stir together shrimp bisque, vegetable broth, rice pilaf mix, celery, onion, and peas until thoroughly combined.

2. Cover and cook on HIGH heat setting for 2 hours. (Rice should be slightly wet.) Stir in shrimp. Cover and cook for 20 to 30 minutes more or until shrimp is heated through.

3. Serve with chopped parsley and lemon wedges (optional).

Lemony Rice with Shrimp and Spinach

Prep 20 minutes
Cook HIGH 3 hours
Makes 6 servings

3	cups water
1	bag (14-ounce) frozen cooked medium shrimp
2	cups converted long-grain rice, *Uncle Ben's*®
1	container (8-ounce) frozen fish stock, thawed, *Perfect Addition*®
1	bottle (8-ounce) clam juice, *Snow's*®
1	can (6-ounce) hollandaise sauce, *Aunt Penny's*®
3	tablespoons bottled lemon juice, *ReaLemon*®
1	package (10-ounce) frozen chopped spinach, *C&W*®
	Grated Parmesan cheese, *DiGiorno*®

1. In a 5-quart slow cooker, stir together water, shrimp, rice, fish stock, clam juice, hollandaise sauce, and lemon juice until thoroughly combined.

2. Cover and cook on HIGH heat setting for 3 hours.

3. To serve, place spinach in a microwave-safe bowl. Cover and microwave on high setting (100% power) for 6 to 8 minutes. Drain. Let stand until cool enough to handle; squeeze out excess liquid. Stir spinach into rice mixture in slow cooker.

4. Serve with Parmesan cheese.

Poultry

Chicken is the "Miss Congeniality" of the food world. It goes anywhere, feeds anyone, and is good in just about anything. Everybody likes chicken. And anybody can make it. This chapter offers 15 creative options for roasting, braising, stuffing, and saucing all kinds of poultry. You'll find Honeyed Thighs, Ginger Chicken, and Cherry Chai Chicken, slow cooked all day until they're fork tender. You'll find chicken alternatives, like feisty Kung Pao Game Hens, creamy Turkey Fricassee, and elegant Turkey with Cranberry-Merlot Sauce, each marinated in deftly seasoned juices to mellow out that "gamey" taste. Get them started in the morning, then finish them off whenever you want. Have them for lunch or dinner, save them for the next day, snack on them all week, or freeze them for later. Just simmer and serve. It's cooking made so simple, the hardest thing about it is deciding which dish to choose.

The Recipes

Chicken with Bacon, Mushrooms, and Onions

Prep 15 minutes
Cook LOW 3 to 5 hours
Makes 6 servings

2	pounds boneless, skinless chicken breast halves, cut into 1-inch pieces
1	package (8-ounce) presliced fresh mushrooms
1½	cups frozen loose-pack petite pearl onions, *C&W*®
1	can (10.75-ounce) condensed cream of mushroom soup with roasted garlic, *Campbell's*®
¾	cup Chardonnay or other white wine
8	slices precooked bacon, cut into ½-inch pieces, *Hormel*®
1	tablespoon fines herbes, *Spice Islands*®
2	teaspoons bottled crushed garlic, *Christopher Ranch*®
	Hot mashed potatoes (optional)

1. In a 4- to 5-quart slow cooker, stir together chicken, mushrooms, onions, soup, wine, bacon, fines herbes, and garlic until thoroughly combined.

2. Cover and cook on LOW heat setting for 3 to 5 hours.

3. Serve with mashed potatoes (optional).

Arroz con Pollo

Prep 15 minutes
Cook HIGH 2 hours
Makes 6 servings

1½	pounds boneless, skinless chicken breast halves, cut into bite-size pieces
3	cups reduced-sodium chicken broth, *Swanson*®
1	can (14.5-ounce) diced tomatoes with green chiles, *S&W*®
2	bags (5 ounces each) saffron yellow rice, *Mahatma*®
1	cup frozen chopped onion, *Ore-Ida*®
1	cup dry sherry, *Christian Brothers*®
½	cup pimiento-stuffed green olives, sliced, *Early California*®

1. In a 4- to 5-quart slow cooker, stir together chicken, chicken broth, undrained tomatoes, rice, onion, sherry, and olives until thoroughly combined.

2. Cover and cook on HIGH heat setting for 2 hours or until chicken is cooked. (Rice should be slightly wet.)

Coq au Vin

Prep 15 minutes
Cook LOW 5 to 6 hours
Makes 6 servings

"Coq au Vin" is French for chicken with wine. Use a fruity, full-bodied wine and serve with steamed potatoes to mop up the gravy. The flavor deepens after a couple of days in the fridge, so save some for leftovers.

2	pounds boneless, skinless chicken breast halves, cut into 1-inch pieces
2	medium red bell peppers, cut into strips
2	cups Merlot or other red wine
1	cup frozen loose-pack petite white onions, *C&W*®
1	cup frozen loose-pack sliced carrots
1	rib celery, chopped
1	can (6-ounce) tomato paste, *Hunt's*®
¼	cup cognac
2	strips precooked bacon, cut into 1-inch pieces, *Hormel*®
2	tablespoons zesty herb marinade mix, *McCormick*®

1. In a 4- to 5-quart slow cooker, stir together chicken, pepper strips, wine, onions, carrots, celery, tomato paste, cognac, bacon, and herb marinade mix until thoroughly combined.

2. Cover and cook on LOW heat setting for 5 to 6 hours.

Honeyed Thighs

Prep 20 minutes
Cook LOW 4 to 6 hours
Makes 4 servings

2½	pounds chicken thighs
	Salt and ground black pepper
1	package (10-ounce) frozen honey-glazed carrots, *Green Giant*®
1	cup frozen chopped onion, *Ore-Ida*®
½	cup dried apricots, *Sun-Maid*®
½	cup golden raisins, *Sun-Maid*®
¼	cup honey, *SueBee*®
1	teaspoon salt-free garlic-and-herb seasoning, *McCormick*®

1. Preheat broiler. Line a baking sheet with aluminum foil; set aside. Trim fat from chicken. Place chicken thighs, skin sides up, on prepared baking sheet. Sprinkle with salt and pepper. Broil 6 inches from heat for 10 minutes or until skin is golden and begins to crisp.*

2. In a 4-quart slow cooker, combine carrots, onion, apricots, and raisins. Add chicken. Pour honey over chicken; sprinkle with garlic-and-herb seasoning.

3. Cover and cook on LOW heat setting for 4 to 6 hours.

*Note: This step may be omitted, but it produces a better-flavored dish.

Yogurt-Braised Chicken

Prep 25 minutes
Cook LOW 4 to 6 hours
Makes 6 servings

3	chicken breast halves
6	chicken thighs
	Salt and ground black pepper
1½	cups frozen chopped onion, *Ore-Ida*®
1½	cups plain nonfat yogurt, *Alta Dena*®
1	tablespoon garam masala, *McCormick*®
1½	teaspoons poppy seeds, *McCormick*®
1	cup sour cream, *Knudsen*®
	Chopped fresh herbs (optional)

1. Preheat broiler. Line a baking sheet with aluminum foil; set aside. Trim fat from chicken. Cut breast halves in half crosswise. Sprinkle with salt and pepper. Arrange chicken pieces on prepared baking sheet, skin sides up. Broil 6 inches from heat for 10 minutes or until skin is golden and begins to crisp.*

2. Place onion in a 5-quart slow cooker. Add chicken. In a small bowl, stir together yogurt, garam masala, and poppy seeds. Pour over chicken.

3. Cover and cook on LOW heat setting for 4 to 6 hours.

4. Transfer chicken to a serving platter. Carefully pour 2 cups of the cooking juices into a blender. Add sour cream. Cover; place a kitchen towel over lid. Blend until mixture is smooth.

5. Spoon yogurt mixture over chicken. Sprinkle with fresh herbs (optional).

*Note: This step may be omitted, but it produces a better-flavored dish.

Tagine of Chicken

Prep 15 minutes
Cook LOW 3 to 5 hours
Makes 6 servings

A Moroccan tagine refers to a spiced stew and the pot it's cooked in.
Here a sensuous mingling of ginger, garlic, lemons, and olives makes chicken
ladled over couscous tempt smell, sight, and taste.

2	pounds boneless, skinless chicken breast halves, cut into bite-size pieces
1	cup green olives, *Star*®
¾	cup reduced-sodium chicken broth, *Swanson*®
½	medium onion, sliced
1	tablespoon bottled chopped ginger, *Christopher Ranch*®
1	tablespoon bottled lemon juice, *ReaLemon*®
2	teaspoons garam masala, *McCormick*®
2	teaspoons bottled crushed garlic, *Christopher Ranch*®
1	teaspoon salt-free lemon pepper, *McCormick*®
½	teaspoon ground turmeric, *McCormick*®
	Hot cooked couscous (optional)

1. In a 4-quart slow cooker, stir together chicken, olives, chicken broth, onion, ginger, lemon juice, garam masala, garlic, lemon pepper, and turmeric until thoroughly combined.

2. Cover and cook on LOW heat setting for 3 to 5 hours.

3. Serve with cooked couscous (optional).

Cherry Chai Chicken

Prep 30 minutes
Cook LOW 4 to 6 hours
Makes 4 servings

2½   pounds chicken thighs
      Salt and ground black pepper
1   cup frozen pitted cherries, *Dole*®
½   cup frozen chopped onion, *Ore-Ida*®
2   chai spice tea bags, *Stash Tea*®
½   cup cherry preserves, *Smucker's*®
½   cup port wine, *Hard's*®
      Hot cooked egg noodles (optional)

1. Preheat broiler. Line a baking sheet with aluminum foil; set aside. Trim fat from chicken. Place chicken thighs, skin sides up, on prepared baking sheet. Sprinkle with salt and pepper. Broil 6 inches from heat for 10 minutes or until skin is golden and begins to crisp.*

2. In a 4- to 5-quart slow cooker, layer cherries, onion, and tea bags. Add chicken. In a small bowl, stir together preserves and wine. Pour over chicken.

3. Cover and cook on LOW heat setting for 4 to 6 hours.

4. Remove chicken to a serving platter; cover with aluminum foil to keep warm. Remove tea bags from slow cooker; transfer cherry mixture to a small saucepan.

5. Over high heat, bring cherry mixture to a boil. Cook until mixture is reduced by half, stirring occasionally.

6. Serve chicken on top of noodles (optional). Spoon cherry mixture over chicken.

*Note: This step may be omitted, but it produces a better-flavored dish.

Asian-Style Chicken and Rice

Prep 20 minutes
Cook HIGH 3 to 4 hours
Makes 6 servings

2	pounds bone-in chicken breast halves
2	stalks lemongrass
2	cans (14 ounces each) reduced-sodium chicken broth, *Swanson®*
1½	cups frozen shelled green soybeans (edamame), thawed, *Seapoint Farms®*
1	cup converted long-grain rice, *Uncle Ben's®*
1	rib celery, sliced diagonally
¼	cup finely chopped fresh cilantro
2	scallions (green onions), sliced diagonally
2	packages (1.25 ounces each) chow mein seasoning mix, *Kikkoman®*

1. Preheat broiler. Line a baking sheet with aluminum foil; set aside. Trim fat from chicken. Place chicken pieces on prepared baking sheet, skin sides up. Broil 4 to 6 inches from heat for 8 to 10 minutes or until skin is golden and begins to crisp.*

2. Peel the tough outer leaves from the lemongrass and cut the stalks into 4-inch-long pieces. With the back of a knife, bruise the lemongrass several times.

3. In a 5-quart slow cooker, stir together lemongrass, chicken broth, soybeans, rice, celery, cilantro, scallions, and chow mein seasoning mix until thoroughly combined. Add chicken.

4. Cover and cook on HIGH heat setting for 3 to 4 hours.

*Note: This step may be omitted, but it produces a better-flavored dish.

Ginger Chicken

Prep 20 minutes
Cook LOW 3 to 5 hours
Makes 6 servings

3	chicken breast halves
6	chicken thighs
	Salt and ground black pepper
1	jar (12-ounce) ginger preserves, *Robertson's*®
1	cup frozen chopped onion, *Ore-Ida*®
2	tablespoons soy sauce, *Kikkoman*®
2	teaspoons bottled crushed garlic, *Christopher Ranch*®
	Hot cooked pasta (optional)

1. Preheat broiler. Line a baking sheet with aluminum foil; set aside. Sprinkle chicken with salt and pepper. Cut chicken breast halves in half crosswise. Arrange chicken pieces on prepared baking sheet, skin sides up. Broil 4 to 6 inches from heat for 10 to 12 minutes or until skin is golden and begins to crisp.*

2. In a medium bowl, combine preserves, onion, soy sauce, and garlic.

3. Place a layer of chicken in a 5-quart slow cooker. Top with half of the preserves mixture. Repeat layers.

4. Cover and cook on LOW heat setting for 3 to 5 hours.

5. Serve over cooked pasta (optional).

*Note: This step may be omitted, but it produces a better-flavored dish.

Kung Pao Game Hens

Prep 20 minutes
Cook LOW 4 to 6 hours
Makes 6 servings

3	Cornish game hens
	Garlic salt and ground black pepper
2	medium red bell peppers, cut into strips
1	medium green bell pepper, cut into strips
1	medium onion, sliced
¼	cup sherry, *Christian Brothers*®
1	packet (1.5-ounce) teriyaki sauce mix, *Kikkoman*®
1	tablespoon Szechuan seasoning, *McCormick*®
1	cup cocktail peanuts, *Planters*®

1. Preheat broiler. Line a baking sheet with aluminum foil; set aside. Using kitchen scissors, cut backbones from game hens. Cut game hens in half through breastbones.

2. Place hen halves on prepared baking sheet, skin sides up. Sprinkle with garlic salt and black pepper. Broil 6 to 8 inches from heat for 10 to 12 minutes or until skin is golden and begins to crisp.*

3. In a 5- to 6-quart slow cooker, combine bell pepper strips and onion. Add game hens. In a small bowl, combine sherry, teriyaki sauce mix, and Szechuan seasoning. Pour over game hens. Sprinkle with peanuts.

4. Cover and cook on LOW heat setting for 4 to 6 hours.

5. Transfer hens to a serving platter. Using a slotted spoon, remove vegetables and peanuts from slow cooker to serve with hens.

*Note: This step may be omitted but it produces a better-flavored dish.

Currant-Glazed
Game Hens

Prep 30 minutes
Cook LOW 5 to 5½ hours
Makes 6 servings

3   **Cornish game hens**
     Salt and ground black pepper
1   **jar (10- to 12-ounce) red currant jelly,** *Knott's Berry Farm*®
2   **teaspoons salt-free chicken seasoning,** *McCormick*®
1   **recipe Currant Stuffing (optional)**

1. To broil hens,* preheat broiler. Line a baking sheet or broiler pan with aluminum foil; set aside. Cut backbones from game hens with kitchen shears. Cut hens in half through breastbones.

2. Place hens, skin sides up, on prepared baking sheet. Season with salt and pepper. Broil 6 to 8 inches from the heat for 10 to 12 minutes or until skin is golden and begins to crisp.

3. In a small saucepan, melt jelly over medium-low heat. Stir in chicken seasoning; divide mixture in half. Cover and chill 1 portion. Brush the remaining half of the melted jelly mixture onto game hens. Arrange hens, skin sides up, in a 4½- or 5-quart slow cooker. Cover and cook on LOW heat setting for 5 to 5½ hours if hens were broiled and 5½ to 6 hours if hens were not broiled.

4. Prepare Currant Stuffing (optional). Transfer hens to a serving platter. Reheat the reserved chilled jelly mixture over medium-low heat until melted; brush over game hens. Serve with Currant Stuffing (optional).

Currant Stuffing: Prepare 1 box (6-ounce) traditional sage stuffing mix (*Stove Top*®) according to package directions. Stir in ⅓ cup chopped pecans (*Diamond*®), toasted if desired, and ¼ cup dried currants (*Sun-Maid*®).

*Note: This step may be omitted, but it produces a better-flavored dish.

Turkey in Mustard Cream Sauce

Prep 15 minutes
Cook LOW 4 to 6 hours
Makes 6 servings

2	pounds boneless, skinless turkey breast
	Salt and ground black pepper
1	cup frozen chopped onion, *Ore-Ida*®
2	cups Chardonnay or other white wine
⅓	cup Dijon mustard, *Grey Poupon*®
1	packet (1.8-ounce) white sauce mix, *Knorr*®
2	teaspoons herbes de Provence, *McCormick*®

1. Sprinkle turkey with salt and pepper.

2. Place onion in a 5-quart slow cooker. Place turkey on top.

3. In a medium bowl, stir together wine, mustard, white sauce mix, and herbes de Provence. Pour over turkey and onion.

4. Cover and cook on LOW heat setting for 4 to 6 hours.

5. Remove turkey to a cutting board and tent with aluminum foil. Let stand for 5 minutes; slice.

6. Using a wire mesh strainer, strain cooking juices into a serving bowl (optional). Serve over sliced turkey.

Turkey with Cranberry-Merlot Sauce

Prep 10 minutes
Cook LOW 4 to 6 hours
Makes 6 servings

2	pounds boneless, skinless turkey breast
¾	teaspoon garlic salt, *Lawry's*®
1	cup frozen chopped onion, *Ore-Ida*®
1	can (16-ounce) whole cranberry sauce, *Ocean Spray*®
1	cup Merlot or other red wine
1	packet (1-ounce) peppercorn sauce mix, *Knorr*®

1. Sprinkle turkey with garlic salt; set aside.

2. Place onion in a 5-quart slow cooker. Place turkey on top. In a medium bowl, stir together cranberry sauce, wine, and peppercorn sauce mix. Pour over turkey.

3. Cover and cook on LOW heat setting for 4 to 6 hours.

4. Slice turkey and serve with cooking juices.

Turkey Fricassee

Prep 15 minutes
Cook LOW 3½ to 5 hours
Makes 6 servings

2	pounds boneless, skinless turkey breast, cut into bite-size pieces
1	can (10.75-ounce) condensed cream of celery soup, *Campbell's*®
1	cup frozen loose-pack sliced carrots, *C&W*®
1	cup frozen loose-pack petite peas, *C&W*®
1	cup frozen chopped onion, *Ore-Ida*®
2	ribs celery, diced
1	cup Chardonnay or other white wine
1	packet (0.87-ounce) turkey gravy mix, *McCormick*®
	Mashed potatoes or hot cooked egg noodles (optional)

1. In a 4-quart slow cooker, stir together turkey, soup, carrots, peas, onion, celery, wine, and gravy mix until thoroughly combined.

2. Cover and cook on LOW heat setting for 3½ to 5 hours.

3. Serve over cooked mashed potatoes or egg noodles (optional).

Champagne Turkey

Prep 15 minutes
Cook LOW 3½ to 5 hours
Makes 6 servings

If you think slow cooking lacks sparkle, try a turkey dish that bubbles with sophistication. Dry champagne and fresh fennel make a slightly sweet white sauce that's a festive break from traditional brown gravy.

2	pounds boneless, skinless turkey breast, cut into 1-inch pieces
1	package (8-ounce) presliced fresh mushrooms
1	fennel bulb, stems removed, quartered, and sliced
1	cup frozen chopped onion, *Ore-Ida®*
2	ribs celery, sliced
1	cup reduced-sodium chicken broth, *Swanson®*
½	cup extra-dry champagne, *Korbel®*
1	packet (1.8-ounce) white sauce mix, *Knorr®*
1	teaspoon dried thyme, *McCormick®*
	Wild rice pilaf or hot cooked rice (optional)

1. In a 4- to 5-quart slow cooker, stir together turkey, mushrooms, fennel, onion, celery, chicken broth, champagne, white sauce mix, and thyme until thoroughly combined.

2. Cover and cook on LOW heat setting for 3½ to 5 hours.

3. Serve over wild rice pilaf or cooked rice (optional).

Meats

I was scraping beef tendons at Le Cordon Bleu, surrounded by a battalion of pots, and I thought, "There's no way." The meal might be perfection on a plate, but it just wasn't doable for the average person. Meat in the slow cooker is the best of both worlds—cooked slow, but ready fast, with a deep, simmered-in taste that takes hours to acquire. Inexpensive, tough cuts of meat cook juicy and tender, steeped in sauces from old-fashioned barbecue to trendy mango-chipotle. Whether you're looking for down home on the range or chic in the city, this chapter offers it all. Choose campfire classics such as Sausage with Four Beans or impress-your-friends favorites like Szechuan Ribs and Pork Bolognese. Either way, serve them straight from the pot, ladling broth over the top for sauce. One meal, one pot. That's doable and delicious.

The Recipes

Creamy Steak alla Vodka

Prep 15 minutes
Cook LOW 10 to 12 hours
Makes 6 servings

2½ pounds beef round steak
1 package (8-ounce) presliced fresh mushrooms
1 medium onion, chopped
1 can (10.75-ounce) condensed cream of mushroom soup with roasted garlic, *Campbell's®*
1 cup tomato-based pasta sauce, *Prego®*
¼ cup vodka
¼ cup reduced-sodium beef broth, *Swanson®*
2 teaspoons dried Italian seasoning, *McCormick®*

1. Cut steak into 6 serving-size portions; set aside.

2. In a 4-quart slow cooker, combine mushrooms and onion. Add steak.

3. For sauce, in a medium bowl, combine soup, pasta sauce, vodka, beef broth, and Italian seasoning; pour over steak.

4. Cover and cook on LOW heat setting for 10 to 12 hours.

5. Serve steak with sauce.

Hunter's Steak

Prep 15 minutes
Cook LOW 8 to 10 hours
Makes 6 servings

2½ pounds beef round steak
1 can (28-ounce) whole peeled tomatoes, *Progresso®*
1 package (8-ounce) presliced fresh mushrooms
1 cup frozen loose-pack sliced carrots, *C&W®*
2 ribs celery, sliced
1½ cups reduced-sodium beef broth, *Swanson®*
1 cup condensed cream of mushroom soup, *Campbell's®*
1 packet (1.5-ounce) beef stew seasoning mix, *McCormick®*
Hot cooked egg noodles (optional)

1. Cut steak into 6 serving-size portions; set aside.

2. In a 5-quart slow cooker, combine undrained tomatoes, mushrooms, carrots, and celery. Place steak on top of vegetables.

3. In a medium bowl, whisk together beef broth, soup, and beef stew seasoning mix. Pour over steak.

4. Cover and cook on LOW heat setting for 8 to 10 hours.

5. Serve with cooked egg noodles (optional).

Sauerbraten

Prep 25 minutes
Cook LOW 10 to 12 hours
Makes 8 servings

1	**4-pound beef rump roast**
	Ground black pepper
1	**cup frozen chopped onion, *Ore-Ida*®**
2	**ribs celery, diced**
1	**teaspoon bottled crushed garlic, *Christopher Ranch*®**
1	**can (15-ounce) tomato sauce, *Hunt's*®**
1	**can (10-ounce) condensed French onion soup, *Campbell's*®**
¼	**cup red wine vinegar, *Pompeian*®**
1	**packet (1.5-ounce) beef stew seasoning mix, *Lawry's*®**
1	**tablespoon packed brown sugar, *C&H*®**
¾	**cup crushed gingersnaps, *Nabisco*®**

1. Sprinkle roast with pepper; set aside.

2. In a 5-quart slow cooker, combine onion, celery, and garlic. Place roast, fat side up, on top of vegetables.

3. In a medium bowl, combine tomato sauce, soup, vinegar, beef stew seasoning mix, and brown sugar. Pour over roast.

4. Cover and cook on LOW heat setting for 10 to 12 hours.

5. Transfer roast to a cutting board; cover with aluminum foil to keep warm. Let stand for 15 minutes.

6. Meanwhile, turn slow cooker to HIGH heat setting. Stir in gingersnaps; heat until gravy thickens.

7. Slice roast and transfer to serving platter. Pour some of the gravy over roast. Serve with additional gravy.

Mango-Chipotle Pot Roast

Prep 15 minutes
Cook LOW 8 to 10 hours
Makes 6 servings

Caribbean mango meets Southwest chipotle in a complex communing of cultures that meshes delightfully in pot roast. Moist-heat stewing—like smoking—brings out the flavor of the meat.

1	3- to 4-pound boneless beef chuck roast
1	tablespoon Montreal steak seasoning, *McCormick*®
1	package (16-ounce) frozen mango chunks, *Dole*®
2	medium red bell peppers, sliced into $\frac{1}{2}$-inch strips
1	medium onion, sliced
1	jar (16-ounce) chipotle salsa, *Pace*®
1	can (11.5-ounce) mango nectar, *Kern's*®
	Hot cooked orzo or egg noodles (optional)

1. Sprinkle roast with steak seasoning.

2. In a 5-quart slow cooker, combine mango, bell peppers, and onion. Place roast on top of fruit and vegetables.

3. In a small bowl, combine salsa and mango nectar. Pour over roast.

4. Cover and cook on LOW heat setting for 8 to 10 hours.

5. Transfer roast and $\frac{1}{2}$ of the mango and vegetables to a serving platter. Cover with aluminum foil to keep warm.

6. Transfer remaining mixture in slow cooker to a blender. Cover; place a kitchen towel over lid. Blend until smooth.* Serve with roast and reserved vegetables. Serve with hot cooked orzo or egg noodles (optional).

*Note: If you prefer, use a handheld immersion blender to blend the sauce right in the slow cooker.

Beef Fajitas Corona®

Prep 20 minutes
Cook LOW 8 to 10 hours
Makes 6 servings

2½	pounds beef round steaks
2	packets (1.27 ounces each) fajita seasoning mix, *Lawry's®*
2	medium red bell peppers, sliced into ½-inch strips
1	medium green bell pepper, sliced into ½-inch strips
1	medium onion, thickly sliced
½	cup beer, *Corona®*
	Warmed flour tortillas, *Mission®* (optional)

1. Sprinkle steak pieces with 1 packet of the fajita seasoning mix. Roll steak pieces from short ends and secure with 100%-cotton kitchen string; set aside.

2. In a 5-quart slow cooker, toss together bell pepper strips, onion, and remaining packet of fajita seasoning mix. Place rolled steaks on top of vegetables. Pour in beer.

3. Cover and cook on LOW heat setting for 8 to 10 hours.

4. Transfer steaks to a cutting board; slice. Using a slotted spoon, transfer vegetables to a serving bowl. Serve steak slices with vegetables in warmed tortillas (optional).

Marmalade Meatballs

Prep 10 minutes
Cook HIGH 2 to 3 hours
Makes 48 meatballs

2	pounds fully cooked frozen meatballs, *Armanino®*
1	bottle (16-ounce) Catalina salad dressing, *Kraft®*
1	cup orange marmalade, *Smucker's®*
3	tablespoons Worcestershire sauce, *Lea & Perrins®*
¾	teaspoon red pepper flakes, *McCormick®*

1. Place frozen meatballs in a 5-quart slow cooker.

2. In a medium bowl, stir together salad dressing, marmalade, Worcestershire sauce, and red pepper flakes. Pour over meatballs, stirring to coat.

3. Cover and cook on HIGH heat setting for 2 to 3 hours.

4. Serve as an appetizer or a main dish.*

*Note: If serving as a main dish, serve over hot cooked rice.

Hungarian Veal

Prep 10 minutes
Cook LOW 8 to 10 hours
Makes 6 servings

The secret to authentic Hungarian goulash is slow cooking and plenty of paprika. Use Hungarian paprika—it's sweeter—and buy the mushrooms presliced.

2½ pounds veal stew meat or veal roast, cut into bite-size pieces
1 package (8-ounce) presliced fresh mushrooms
1 cup frozen chopped onion, *Ore-Ida*®
1 cup frozen loose-pack crinkle-cut sliced carrots, *Pictsweet*®
1 cup reduced-sodium chicken broth, *Swanson*®
2 packages (0.75 ounces each) mushroom gravy mix, *McCormick*®
2 tablespoons Hungarian sweet paprika, *Pride of Szeged*®
1 teaspoon bottled crushed garlic, *Christopher Ranch*®
  Hot cooked egg noodles (optional)
  Fresh herbs sprigs (optional)

1. In a 4- to 5-quart slow cooker, stir together veal, mushrooms, onion, carrots, chicken broth, gravy mix, paprika, and garlic.

2. Cover and cook on LOW heat setting for 8 to 10 hours.

3. Serve over cooked egg noodles and top with herb sprigs (optional).

Curried Lamb and Potatoes

Prep 15 minutes
Cook LOW 6 to 8 hours
Makes 6 servings

$1\frac{1}{2}$ pounds lamb stew meat, cut into bite-size pieces
1   pound small red potatoes, quartered
2   cans (14 ounces each) light coconut milk, *A Taste of Thai*®
1   can (14.5-ounce) diced tomatoes, *Hunt's*®
1   cup frozen loose-pack sliced carrots, *C&W*®
1   cup unsweetened applesauce, *Mott's*®
2   tablespoons curry powder, *Spice Islands*®
1   tablespoon garam masala, *Spice Hunter*® (optional)*
  Hot cooked rice (optional)
  Chopped fresh cilantro (optional)

1. In a 4-quart slow cooker, stir together lamb, potatoes, coconut milk, undrained tomatoes, carrots, applesauce, curry powder, and garam masala until thoroughly combined.

2. Cover and cook on LOW heat setting for 6 to 8 hours.

3. Serve over cooked rice (optional). Sprinkle with cilantro (optional).

*Note: This ingredient is optional, but it gives the dish a fuller flavor.

Pomegranate Lamb

Prep 20 minutes
Cook LOW 5 to 7 hours
Makes 6 servings

1	3½-pound boneless lamb leg roast
12	bottled prepeeled whole garlic cloves, *Christopher Ranch*®
	Salt and ground black pepper
1½	cups pomegranate juice, *Pom Wonderful*®
½	cup Merlot or other red wine
2	tablespoons tomato paste, *Hunt's*®
2	teaspoons herbes de Provence, *McCormick*®
1	package (14-ounce) frozen loose-pack petite pearl onions, *C&W*®
	Fresh pomegranate seeds (optional)

1. Using the tip of a sharp knife, cut slits in roast. Insert whole garlic cloves into slits. Sprinkle roast with salt and pepper; set aside.

2. In a medium bowl, combine pomegranate juice, wine, tomato paste, and herbes de Provence; set aside.

3. Place onions in a 5-quart slow cooker. Place roast on top of onions. Pour pomegranate juice mixture over roast.

4. Cover and cook on LOW heat setting for 5 to 7 hours or until an instant-read thermometer inserted into center of roast reaches 155 degrees F.

5. Transfer roast to a cutting board; tent with aluminum foil to keep warm. Using a slotted spoon, transfer onions to a serving bowl.

6. Skim fat from cooking juices. Using a wire mesh strainer, strain cooking juices into a medium saucepan. Over high heat, bring to a boil. Cook for 5 to 7 minutes or until reduced by half. Serve with roast and onions.

7. Sprinkle with pomegranate seeds (optional).

Zinfandel-Braised Pork Loin

Prep 25 minutes
Cook LOW 6 to 8 hours
Makes 8 servings

1	3½-pound double pork loin roast
1	packet (1.12-ounce) Italian herb marinade mix, *Durkee*®
2	medium tart apples, cored and thickly sliced
1	large onion, thickly sliced
1½	cups Zinfandel or other red wine

1. Sprinkle roast with marinade mix; set aside.

2. In a 5-quart slow cooker, combine apples and onion. Add wine. Place roast on top of onion and apples.

3. Cover and cook on LOW heat setting for 6 to 8 hours.

4. Transfer roast to a cutting board; cover with aluminum foil to keep warm. Let stand for 5 to 10 minutes before slicing. Using a slotted spoon, transfer onion and apples to a serving bowl.

5. Using a wire mesh strainer, strain cooking juices into a medium saucepan. Over high heat, bring to a boil. Cook until mixture is reduced by half. Serve with roast, onion, and apples.

Pork Roast in Two Wines

Prep 25 minutes
Cook LOW 6 to 8 hours
Makes 6 servings

1	3-pound pork shoulder roast
1	packet (1-ounce) peppercorn sauce mix, *Knorr*®
1	cup frozen chopped onion, *Ore-Ida*®
2	ribs celery, cut into pieces
1	cup frozen loose-pack sliced carrots, *C&W*®
1	teaspoon bottled crushed garlic, *Christopher Ranch*®
1	cup Merlot or other red wine,
½	cup Marsala wine, *Lombardo*®
2	tablespoons Dijon mustard, *Grey Poupon*®
	Hot cooked egg noodles (optional)

1. Sprinkle roast with some of the peppercorn sauce mix; set aside.

2. In a 5-quart slow cooker, combine onion, celery, carrots, and garlic. Place roast on top of vegetables. Add remaining peppercorn sauce mix. In a medium bowl, combine red wine, Marsala wine, and mustard. Pour over roast.

3. Cover and cook on LOW heat setting for 6 to 8 hours.

4. Transfer roast to a cutting board; tent with aluminum foil to keep warm. Using a wire mesh strainer, strain cooking juices into a small saucepan. Discard vegetables. Over high heat, bring to a boil; cook until reduced by half.

5. Slice roast. Serve with cooking juices over cooked noodles (optional).

Pork Bolognese

Prep 30 minutes
Cook LOW 7½ to 9½ hours; plus 30 minutes on HIGH
Makes 8 servings

A good Bolognese sauce requires hours of simmering, which would make it high maintenance without a slow cooker. For a spiffier presentation, serve it over wide pappardelle noodles.

1	pound ground pork
2	pounds pork tenderloin, cut into bite-size pieces
1	can (28-ounce) whole peeled tomatoes with basil, broken up, *Progresso®*
1	jar (26-ounce) marinara sauce, *Classico®*
1	cup frozen chopped onion, *Ore-Ida®*
1	cup reduced-sodium beef broth, *Swanson®*
½	cup diced celery
½	cup diced carrots
4	bottled prepeeled whole garlic cloves, *Christopher Ranch®*
1	pound dried linguine, *Barilla®*
¾	cup half-and-half
	Shredded Parmesan cheese, *Kraft®* (optional)

1. In a large skillet, over medium heat, cook and stir ground pork until browned, breaking up clumps. Drain off fat.

2. In a 5-quart slow cooker, stir together browned pork, pork pieces, undrained tomatoes, marinara sauce, onion, beef broth, celery, carrots, and garlic until thoroughly combined.

3. Cover and cook on LOW heat setting for 7½ to 9½ hours.

4. Turn slow cooker to HIGH heat setting; remove lid to help thicken sauce. Cook for 30 minutes more.

5. In a large pot of salted, boiling water, cook linguine according to package directions. Drain; return to hot pot. Keep warm.

6. Skim off any fat or excess moisture that rises to the top of mixture in slow cooker. Stir half-and-half into mixture in slow cooker. Serve over cooked linguine. Sprinkle with Parmesan cheese (optional).

Szechuan Ribs

Prep 10 minutes
Cook LOW 6 to 8 hours
Makes 6 servings

4	pounds pork spare ribs, cut into single-rib portions
1	bottle (20-ounce) hoisin sauce, *Lee Kum Kee*®
½	cup apricot preserves, *Smucker's*®
3	scallions (green onions), chopped
2	tablespoons toasted sesame seeds, *Sun Luck*®
2	tablespoons Szechuan seasoning, *McCormick*®
1	tablespoon bottled chopped ginger, *Christopher Ranch*®

1. Place ribs in a 5-quart slow cooker.

2. In a medium bowl, combine hoisin sauce, preserves, scallions, sesame seeds, Szechuan seasoning, and ginger. Pour over ribs, stirring to coat.

3. Cover and cook on LOW heat setting for 6 to 8 hours.

Sausage with Caramelized Onions and Tomatoes

Prep 10 minutes
Cook LOW 4 to 6 hours; plus 2 hours on HIGH
Makes 6 servings

3	large sweet onions, cut into ½-inch slices
½	stick (¼ cup) butter, cut into chunks
1½	pounds sweet Italian sausage links
¼	cup balsamic vinaigrette salad dressing, *Newman's Own*®
2	cans (14.5 ounces each) Italian stewed tomatoes, drained, *S&W*®
	Hot dog buns

1. Place onions in a 4-quart slow cooker. Dot with butter. Cover and cook on LOW heat setting for 4 to 6 hours.

2. Turn slow cooker to HIGH heat setting. Add sausage and salad dressing. Pour tomatoes on top. Cover and cook for 2 hours.

3. Serve sausage and onions in hot dog buns.

Sausage with Four Beans

Prep 10 minutes
Cook HIGH 4 to 5 hours
Makes 6 servings

1	can (28-ounce) whole peeled Italian tomatoes, *Progresso*®
1	can (15-ounce) cannellini beans, rinsed and drained, *Progresso*®
1	can (15-ounce) kidney beans, rinsed and drained, *Bush's*®
1	can (15-ounce) pinto beans, rinsed and drained, *Bush's*®
1	can (15-ounce) butter beans, rinsed and drained, *Sea Side*®
1	cup frozen chopped onion, *Ore-Ida*®
4	slices precooked bacon, cut into $\frac{1}{2}$-inch pieces, *Hormel*®
1	packet (0.87-ounce) chicken gravy mix, *McCormick*®
2	teaspoons dried Italian seasoning, *McCormick*®
1$\frac{1}{2}$	pounds sweet Italian sausage links

1. In a 5-quart slow cooker, stir together undrained tomatoes, cannellini beans, kidney beans, pinto beans, butter beans, onion, bacon, gravy mix, and Italian seasoning until thoroughly combined. Push sausage links down into bean mixture.

2. Cover and cook on HIGH heat setting for 4 to 5 hours.

3. Cut sausage into serving-size pieces and serve with bean mixture.

Soups, Stews & Chilies

Soups and stews always stir up memories of childhood—a bowl of comfort when I was home sick from school or winter days when chilly outside meant chili inside. This chapter bubbles with rich chowders, chunky stews, and zesty chilies, all prepped in the morning and left to simmer all day. All-American standbys take on a worldly air—chicken soup made island-style with Thai flavors and coconut, split pea soup spiced up with chipotle salsa, and beef stew deep-flavored and filling with Guinness® beer for broth. There's even Chocolaty Chili for those wanting to drink their cocoa and make a meal with it too. We all have a favorite soup in our past, so get out the slow cooker and "cookoon" with something special. Soups have staying power, so freeze the extra to thaw another day.

The Recipes

Hearty Beef and Barley Soup

Prep 15 minutes
Cook LOW 8 to 10 hours
Makes 6 servings

1½	pounds beef stew meat, cut into 1-inch pieces
4	cans (14 ounces each) reduced-sodium beef broth, *Swanson®*
1	cup frozen chopped onion, *Ore-Ida®*
1	cup baby carrots, sliced ½ inch thick
2	ribs celery, diced
¾	cup pearl barley, *Arrowhead Mills®*
1	packet (1.5-ounce) meat loaf seasoning mix, *McCormick®*

1. In a 4-quart slow cooker, stir together beef stew meat, beef broth, onion, carrots, celery, barley, and meat loaf seasoning mix until thoroughly combined.

2. Cover and cook on LOW heat setting for 8 to 10 hours.

Chipotle Split Pea Soup

Prep 15 minutes
Cook LOW 6 to 8 hours
Makes 8 servings

1	13-ounce fully cooked linguica sausage, *Silva®*
1	pound dried split peas
4	cups reduced-sodium chicken broth, *Swanson®*
3	cups water
1½	cups frozen chopped onion, *Ore-Ida®*
1	cup frozen loose-pack sliced carrots, *C&W®*
1	bottle (8-ounce) chipotle taco sauce, *Ortega®*
1	rib celery, diced
½	teaspoon salt
¼	teaspoon ground black pepper
	Red pepper flakes, *McCormick®*
	Sour cream, *Knudsen®* (optional)
	Crushed tortilla chips, *Tostitos®* (optional)

1. Remove casing from sausage; slice sausage.

2. In a 5-quart slow cooker, stir together sausage, split peas, chicken broth, water, onion, carrots, taco sauce, celery, salt, and black pepper until thoroughly combined.

3. Cover and cook on LOW heat setting for 6 to 8 hours.

4. Serve with red pepper flakes, sour cream, and tortilla chips (optional).

Caribbean Black Bean Soup

Prep 20 minutes
Cook HIGH 4 to 5 hours
Makes 6 servings

3	cans (15 ounces each) low-sodium black beans, rinsed and drained, *S&W®*
2	cans (14 ounces each) reduced-sodium chicken broth, *Swanson®*
2	cans (10 ounces each) diced tomatoes with lime and cilantro, *Ro-Tel®*
1	cup frozen chopped onion, *Ore-Ida®*
½	cup diced carrots
½	cup diced celery
1	tablespoon paprika, *McCormick®*
2	teaspoons ground cumin, *McCormick®*
1	teaspoon bottled crushed garlic, *Christopher Ranch®*
¼	teaspoon ground cloves, *McCormick®*
2	tablespoons balsamic vinegar, *Alessi®*
	Sour cream, *Knudsen®* (optional)
	Fresh cilantro leaves (optional)

1. In a 4-quart slow cooker, stir together beans, chicken broth, undrained tomatoes, onion, carrots, celery, paprika, cumin, garlic, and cloves until thoroughly combined.

2. Cover and cook on HIGH heat setting for 4 to 5 hours.

3. Stir in balsamic vinegar. Serve with sour cream and cilantro leaves (optional).

Thai Chicken Soup

Prep 15 minutes
Cook HIGH 3½ to 4½ hours
Makes 6 servings

1¼	pounds boneless, skinless chicken breast halves, diced
2	cans (14 ounces each) reduced-sodium chicken broth, *Swanson*®
2	cans (14 ounces each) light coconut milk, *A Taste of Thai*®
1	can (15-ounce) straw mushrooms, drained, *Polar*®
3	tablespoons refrigerated chopped lemongrass, *Gourmet Garden*®
1	tablespoon bottled chopped ginger, *Christopher Ranch*®
2	teaspoons Thai seasoning, *Spice Islands*®
2	tablespoons bottled lime juice, *ReaLime*®
2	tablespoons chopped fresh cilantro

1. In a 4-quart slow cooker, stir together chicken, chicken broth, coconut milk, mushrooms, lemongrass, ginger, and Thai seasoning until thoroughly combined.

2. Cover and cook on HIGH heat setting for 3½ to 4½ hours.

3. Stir in lime juice and cilantro.

San Francisco-Style Cioppino

Prep 10 minutes
Cook LOW 4 to 6 hours; plus 30 minutes on HIGH
Makes 6 servings

At restaurants along Fisherman's Wharf, chefs toss in the catch of the day for this classic fish stew. A pound of live littleneck clams and a frozen seafood medley offer a similar extravagance of flavors in this tastes-the-same cioppino.

2	cans (14.5 ounces each) diced tomatoes with onion, celery, and bell pepper, *Hunt's*®
2	bottles (8 ounces each) clam juice, *Snow's*®
2	cups white wine, Chardonnay
1	cup frozen chopped onion, *Ore-Ida*®
1	cup frozen chopped bell pepper, *Pictsweet*®
½	cup finely chopped fresh parsley
2	teaspoons dried Italian seasoning, *McCormick*®
1	teaspoon red pepper flakes, *McCormick*®
1	teaspoon bottled crushed garlic, *Christopher Ranch*®
1	teaspoon salt
1	pound frozen seafood mix, thawed, *Sea Harbor*®
1	pound fresh littleneck clams
	Shredded Parmesan cheese, *Kraft*® (optional)

1. In a 4- to 5-quart slow cooker, stir together undrained tomatoes, clam juice, wine, onion, bell pepper, parsley, Italian seasoning, red pepper flakes, garlic, and salt until thoroughly combined.

2. Cover and cook on LOW heat setting for 4 to 6 hours.

3. Turn slow cooker to HIGH heat setting. Add seafood mix and clams. Cover and cook for 30 to 40 minutes more or until seafood is cooked and clams have opened. Discard any unopened clams.

4. Serve with Parmesan cheese (optional).

Guinness® Beef Stew

Prep 15 minutes
Cook LOW 8 to 10 hours
Makes 6 servings

2 pounds beef stew meat, cut into 1-inch pieces
1 pound red potatoes, diced
1 package (16-ounce) frozen loose-pack crinkle-cut sliced carrots, *C&W®*
1 package (16-ounce) frozen loose-pack petite pearl onions, *C&W®*
1 bottle (12-ounce) stout-style beer, *Guinness®*
1 packet (1-ounce) au jus gravy mix, *McCormick®*
2 tablespoons tomato paste, *Hunt's®*
½ teaspoon ground black pepper

1. In a 5-quart slow cooker, stir together beef stew meat, potatoes, carrots, onions, beer, gravy mix, tomato paste, and pepper until thoroughly combined.

2. Cover and cook on LOW heat setting for 8 to 10 hours.

Brunswick Stew

Prep 15 minutes
Cook LOW 6 to 8 hours
Makes 6 servings

1 3- to 4-pound whole roasted chicken*
1 can (15-ounce) cream-style corn, *Green Giant®*
1 can (14.5-ounce) diced tomatoes, *Hunt's®*
1 jar (14-ounce) marinara sauce, *Prego®*
1 can (14-ounce) reduced-sodium chicken broth, *Swanson®*
1½ cups frozen loose-pack baby lima beans or sliced okra, *Birds Eye®*
8 ounces smoked ham, diced, *Hormel®*
1 cup frozen chopped onion, *Ore-Ida®*
½ teaspoon liquid smoke, *Wright's®*

1. Remove skin and bones from chicken; discard skin and bones. Chop cooked chicken.

2. In a 4- to 5-quart slow cooker, stir together chicken, corn, undrained tomatoes, marinara sauce, chicken broth, lima beans or okra, ham, onion, and liquid smoke until thoroughly combined.

3. Cover and cook on LOW heat setting for 6 to 8 hours.

*Note: Pick up a whole roasted chicken at your supermarket's deli counter.

Lemon Chicken Stew

Prep 15 minutes
Cook LOW 4 hours
Makes 6 servings

2	pounds boneless, skinless chicken breast halves, cut into 1-inch pieces
1½	cups reduced-sodium chicken broth, *Swanson®*
1	can (10.75-ounce) condensed cream of potato soup, *Campbell's®*
1	package (8-ounce) frozen artichoke hearts, *C&W®*
1	cup baby carrots, cut into chunks
¾	cup lemon curd, *Dickinson's®*
¼	cup converted long-grain rice, *Uncle Ben's®*
2	teaspoons salt-free lemon pepper seasoning blend, *Mrs. Dash®*
1	teaspoon salt

1. In a 5-quart slow cooker, stir together chicken, chicken broth, soup, artichoke hearts, carrots, lemon curd, rice, lemon pepper seasoning blend, and salt until thoroughly combined.

2. Cover and cook on LOW heat setting for 4 hours.

Seafood Stew

Prep 15 minutes
Cook LOW 6 to 8 hours; plus 30 minutes on HIGH
Makes 6 servings

1½ pounds red potatoes, diced
2 cans (14.5 ounces each) diced tomatoes with onion, celery, and bell pepper, *Hunt's*®
2 cups frozen chopped onion, *Ore-Ida*®
2 bottles (8 ounces each) clam juice, *Snow's*®
1 cup frozen chopped bell pepper, *Pictsweet*®
1 can (6-ounce) tomato paste, *Hunt's*®
⅓ cup chopped fresh parsley
1 box (3-ounce) crab boil, *Zatarain's*®
1 pound frozen seafood mix, thawed, *Sea Harbor*®

1. In a 5-quart slow cooker, stir together potatoes, undrained tomatoes, onion, clam juice, bell pepper, tomato paste, parsley, and crab boil until thoroughly combined.

2. Cover and cook on LOW heat setting for 6 to 8 hours.

3. Turn slow cooker to HIGH heat setting. Add seafood mix. Cover and cook for 30 to 40 minutes more or until seafood is done.

Five-Alarm Three-Bean Chili

Prep 15 minutes
Cook HIGH 4 to 5 hours
Makes 10 servings

2   pounds beef stew meat, cut into small pieces
2   cans (14.5 ounces each) diced tomatoes with zesty green chiles, drained, *Del Monte*®
1   can (15-ounce) pinto beans, rinsed and drained, *Bush's*®
1   can (15-ounce) cannellini beans, rinsed and drained, *Progresso*®
1   can (15-ounce) dark red kidney beans, rinsed and drained, *Bush's*®
1   bottle (12-ounce) ale-style beer
1   medium onion, diced
1   can (6-ounce) tomato paste, *Hunt's*®
2   packets (1.25 ounces each) hot chili seasoning mix, *McCormick*®
2   jalapeño chile peppers, diced*
    Red pepper flakes, *McCormick*®
    Sliced jalapeño chile peppers (optional)

1. In a 5-quart slow cooker, stir together beef stew meat, tomatoes, pinto beans, cannellini beans, kidney beans, beer, onion, tomato paste, chili seasoning mix, diced jalapeño chile peppers, and 2 teaspoons of the red pepper flakes until thoroughly combined.

2. Cover and cook on HIGH heat setting for 4 to 5 hours.

3. Spoon into soup bowls. Top with sliced jalapeño peppers and additional red pepper flakes (optional).

*Note: Because chile peppers contain volatile oils that can burn your skin and eyes, avoid direct contact with them as much as possible. When working with chile peppers, wear plastic or rubber gloves. If your bare hands do touch the peppers, wash your hands and nails well with soap and warm water.

Texas BBQ Chili

Prep 15 minutes
Cook LOW 6 to 8 hours
Makes 6 servings

1   pound lean ground beef
1   pound beef stew meat, cut into bite-size pieces
2   cans (14.5 ounces each) kidney beans, rinsed and drained, *Bush's*®
1   bottle (18-ounce) mesquite-flavor barbecue sauce, *Bull's-Eye*®
1   can (14.5-ounce) diced tomatoes, *Hunt's*®
1   cup frozen chopped onion, *Ore-Ida*®
1   cup frozen chopped bell pepper, *Pictsweet*®
1   can (4-ounce) chopped mild green chile peppers, *La Victoria*®
1   packet (1.25-ounce) hot chili seasoning mix, *McCormick*®
    Chopped onions (optional)
    Shredded pepper Jack cheese (optional)

1. In a large skillet, over high heat, cook and stir ground beef until browned, breaking up clumps. Drain off fat.

2. In a 5-quart slow cooker, stir together browned beef, beef stew meat, kidney beans, barbecue sauce, undrained tomatoes, frozen chopped onion, bell pepper, green chile peppers, and chili seasoning; mix until thoroughly combined.

3. Cover and cook on LOW heat setting for 6 to 8 hours.

4. Serve with chopped onions and shredded cheese (optional).

Santa Fe Chile Verde

Prep 15 minutes
Cook LOW 6 to 8 hours
Makes 6 servings

$2\frac{1}{2}$ pounds pork tenderloin
1   jar (16-ounce) salsa verde, *La Victoria*®
2   cans (7 ounces each) diced mild green chile peppers, *La Victoria*®
1   large onion, chopped
$\frac{1}{2}$ cup gold tequila, *Jose Cuervo*®
2   teaspoons bottled crushed garlic, *Christopher Ranch*®
    Warmed burrito-size flour tortillas, *Mission*® (optional)
    Fresh cilantro sprigs (optional)
    Lime wedges (optional)

1. Trim fat and silver skin from pork; cut into $\frac{1}{2}$-inch pieces.

2. In a 4-quart slow cooker, stir together pork, salsa verde, chile peppers, onion, tequila, and garlic until thoroughly combined.

3. Cover and cook on LOW heat setting for 6 to 8 hours.

4. Serve in warmed tortillas with cilantro sprigs and lime wedges (optional).

Cincinnati-Style Chili

Prep 25 minutes
Cook LOW 8 to 10 hours
Makes 8 servings

My Cincinnati-Style Chili is served "Five-Way"—with kidney beans on top of spaghetti, garnished with mounds of cheese, olives, and onions. The distinctive flavor comes from cocoa powder with a twang of cider vinegar.

- 2½ pounds lean ground beef
- 2 cans (15 ounces each) kidney beans, rinsed and drained, *Bush's*®
- 2 cans (10 ounces each) condensed tomato soup, *Campbell's*®
- 1½ cups frozen chopped onion, *Ore-Ida*®
- 1 cup frozen chopped green bell pepper, *Pictsweet*®
- 2 packets (1.25 ounces each) chili seasoning mix, *McCormick*®
- 2 tablespoons beef stew seasoning mix, *McCormick*®
- 1 tablespoon cider vinegar, *Heinz*®
- 1½ teaspoons unsweetened cocoa powder, *Hershey's*®
- 16 ounces dried spaghetti, *Barilla*®
  Shredded cheddar cheese, *Kraft*® (optional)
  Sliced black olives, *Early California*® (optional)
  Chopped onions (optional)

1. In a large skillet, over high heat, cook and stir ground beef until browned, breaking up clumps. Drain off fat.

2. In 4- to 5-quart slow cooker, stir together beef, beans, soup, frozen chopped onion, bell pepper, chili seasoning mix, beef stew seasoning mix, vinegar, and cocoa powder until thoroughly combined.

3. Cover and cook on LOW heat setting for 8 to 10 hours.

4. In a large pot of salted, boiling water, cook spaghetti according to package directions. Drain. Spoon chili over spaghetti.

5. Serve with shredded cheese, olives, and chopped onions (optional).

Chocolaty Chili

Prep 15 minutes
Cook LOW 4 to 6 hours
Makes 6 servings

1½ pounds ground pork
2 cans (15 ounces each) pinto beans, rinsed and drained, *Bush's®*
1 jar (16-ounce) chipotle salsa, *Pace®*
1¼ cups red wine, Merlot
1 cup frozen chopped onion, *Ore-Ida®*
1 can (4-ounce) diced mild green chile peppers, *La Victoria®*
1 packet (1.25-ounce) chipotle taco seasoning mix, *Ortega®*
3 tablespoons tomato paste, *Hunt's®*
    Unsweetened cocoa powder, *Hershey's®*
3 tablespoons packed brown sugar, *C&H®*
1 teaspoon ground cinnamon, *McCormick®*
    Sour cream, *Knudsen®* (optional)
    Chopped scallions (green onions) (optional)

1. In a large skillet, over high heat, cook and stir ground pork until browned, breaking up clumps. Drain off fat.

2. In a 4- to 5-quart slow cooker, stir together pork, beans, salsa, wine, onion, chile peppers, taco seasoning mix, tomato paste, 3 tablespoons of the cocoa powder, brown sugar, and cinnamon until combined.

3. Cover and cook on LOW heat setting for 4 to 6 hours.

4. Serve with sour cream, scallions, and additional cocoa powder (optional).

White Chili

Prep 15 minutes
Cook LOW 6 to 8 hours
Makes 8 servings

2 pounds boneless, skinless chicken breast halves, cut into ½-inch pieces
2 cans (15 ounces each) cannellini beans, rinsed and drained, *Progresso®*
1 can (15-ounce) cream-style corn, *Green Giant®*
2 cans (4 ounces each) diced mild green chile peppers, *La Victoria®*
1 cup frozen chopped onion, *Ore-Ida®*
1 cup reduced-sodium chicken broth, *Swanson®*
2 packets (1.25 ounces each) white chicken chili seasoning mix, *McCormick®*
    Shredded cheddar cheese, *Kraft®* (optional)
    Chopped green bell pepper (optional)

1. In a 4-quart slow cooker, stir together chicken, beans, corn, chile peppers, onion, chicken broth, and chili seasoning mix until combined. Cover and cook on LOW heat setting for 6 to 8 hours.

2. Serve with cheese and chopped green pepper (optional).

Desserts

Desserts always remind me of my Grandma Lorraine—sifting, stirring, rolling out dough. I shared the secrets of childhood while she shared the secrets of baking. Baking, I learned, is a lot like life. The toughest crust can hide the softest of centers. Tart green apples bake up sweet. Be generous, not just with sugar and spice but also with people. Whether you're baking cookies in an oven—or a cake in the slow cooker—desserts offer a chance to give of yourself. Dessert in the slow cooker is dessert made the decadent way, with ingredients canoodling for hours into a heady rush of flavor. Pears poached in Chianti with sliced orange, white chocolate and cranberry bread pudding bathed in cream, peach pie given a jolt of ginger—all cooked nice and slow—deliver simple and pure delights that prove the sweetest things always come to those who wait.

The Recipes

Coffee 'n' Cream
Streusel Cake

Prep 25 minutes
Cook LOW 3 to 4 hours
Makes 8 servings

	Butter-flavor cooking spray, *Mazola® Pure*
1	box (16-ounce) pound cake mix, *Betty Crocker®*
2	large eggs
¾	cup water
¼	cup plus 2 tablespoons Viennese-style coffee drink mix, *General Foods International®*
¼	cup packed brown sugar, *C&H®*
	Nut topping, *Planters®*
1	tablespoon all-purpose flour

1. Lightly coat a 6-cup soufflé dish with cooking spray. Cut parchment paper to fit the bottom of the soufflé dish. Place in soufflé dish. Coat parchment paper with cooking spray; set aside.

2. In a large mixing bowl, combine cake mix, eggs, water, and ¼ cup of the coffee drink mix. Using a handheld electric mixer, beat on low speed for 3 minutes, scraping down the sides of bowl. Pour into prepared soufflé dish.

3. In a small bowl, combine the remaining 2 tablespoons coffee drink mix, brown sugar, ¼ cup of the nut topping, and flour. Sprinkle over top of cake batter. Using a table knife, lightly swirl topping into batter; set aside.

4. Crumple aluminum foil to create a "ring base" about 5 inches in diameter and 1 inch thick. Place ring in a 5-quart slow cooker. Place soufflé dish on top of ring. Stack 8 paper towels; place on top of slow cooker (to absorb moisture). Secure with lid.

5. Cook on LOW heat setting for 3 to 4 hours. (Do not lift lid for the first 2 hours of cooking.)

6. Transfer soufflé dish to a wire rack; cool completely. Using a thin-bladed knife, loosen edge of cake from dish. Invert onto a serving plate. Sprinkle with additional nut topping (optional).

Chianti-Poached Pears

Prep 20 minutes
Cook LOW 6 to 8 hours
Makes 6 servings

Mulled wine becomes a showpiece dessert when poured over a pear compote. Brown sugar and Chianti give the pears a candied texture during slow cooking. If you like, add vanilla bean ice cream as a crowning glory.

4	under-ripe pears
1	medium orange, sliced
2	tablespoons mulling spices, *Morton & Bassett*®
1	bottle (750 milliliter) Chianti
1	cup packed brown sugar, *C&H*®
	Orange juice or water (optional)
	Blood orange slices (optional)

1. Using a vegetable peeler, peel pears. Cut each pear in half and use a melon baller to remove core. Place in a 4- to 5-quart slow cooker. Add orange slices and mulling spices.

2. In a large bowl, stir together Chianti and brown sugar. Pour over pears. If wine does not cover pears completely, add enough orange juice or water to cover.

3. Cover slow cooker and cook on LOW heat setting for 6 to 8 hours or until pears can be easily pierced with a fork.

4. Serve with blood orange slices (optional).*

*Note: These pears also are delicious sliced and served in a salad.

Tropical Compote

Prep 10 minutes
Cook HIGH 3 to 4 hours
Makes 6 servings

1	bag (16-ounce) frozen mango chunks, *Dole®*
1	bag (16-ounce) frozen pineapple chunks, *Dole®*
1	bag (6-ounce) dried fruit mix (pineapple, papaya, mango), *Mariana®*
½	cup shredded coconut, *Baker's®*
¾	cup mango nectar, *Kern's®*
¼	cup packed brown sugar, *C&H®*
¼	cup spiced rum, *Captain Morgan®*
1	packet (0.74-ounce) spiced cider drink mix, *Alpine®*
	Fresh mint leaves (optional)

1. In a 4-quart slow cooker, stir together mango, pineapple, dried fruit mix, and coconut until thoroughly combined.

2. In a small bowl, stir together mango nectar, brown sugar, rum, and cider drink mix. Pour over fruit mixture, stirring to combine.

3. Cover and cook on HIGH heat setting for 3 to 4 hours.

4. Serve with mint (optional).

Apple-Raisin Betty

Prep 10 minutes
Cook LOW 3 to 4 hours
Makes 10 servings

Butter-flavor cooking spray, *Mazola® Pure*
2   cans (21 ounces each) apple pie filling, ***Comstock® More Fruit***
1   teaspoon ground cinnamon, ***McCormick®***
3   packets (1.51 ounces each) instant oatmeal with raisins
    and spices, ***Quaker®***
6   tablespoons butter
    Vanilla ice cream, ***Häagen-Dazs®*** (optional)

1. Coat a 4-quart slow cooker with cooking spray. Spoon 1 can of apple pie filling into slow cooker. Sprinkle with half of the cinnamon and 1½ of the oatmeal packets. Dot with half of the butter. Repeat layers.

2. Cover and cook on LOW heat setting for 3 to 4 hours.

3. Serve with ice cream (optional).

Blackberry Cobbler

Prep 10 minutes
Cook LOW 4 to 6 hours
Makes 10 servings

Butter-flavor cooking spray, *Mazola® Pure*
2   bags (16 ounces each) frozen blackberries, thawed, ***Dole®***
1   cup sugar
3   tablespoons quick-cooking tapioca, ***Minute®***
1   packet (7.75-ounce) honey butter biscuit mix, ***Bisquick® Complete***
¾   cup cream soda, ***Dad's®***
    Heavy cream (optional)

1. Coat a 4- to 5-quart slow cooker with cooking spray.

2. In a large bowl, combine blackberries, sugar, and tapioca. Transfer to slow cooker. Sprinkle biscuit mix over berries. Slowly pour cream soda over biscuit mix.

3. Cover and cook on LOW heat setting for 4 to 6 hours.

4. Serve warm with cream (optional).

Cherry Crumble

Prep 30 minutes
Cook HIGH 2 to 4 hours
Makes 8 servings

FOR SLOW-COOKED CHERRIES:

1	bag (16-ounce) frozen cherries, *C&W*®
1	cup sugar
¾	cup water
½	cup dried cherries, *Mariani*®
¼	cup cherry brandy
2	tablespoons quick-cooking tapioca, *Minute*®

FOR CRUMBLE TOPPING:

¾	cup low-fat granola, *Quaker*® *100% Natural*
½	cup baking mix, *Bisquick*®
10	gingersnaps, crushed, *Nabisco*®
2	tablespoons butter, melted
	Vanilla ice cream, *Häagen-Dazs*®

1. For Slow-Cooked Cherries, in a 4-quart slow cooker, stir together frozen cherries, sugar, water, dried cherries, brandy, and tapioca. Cover and cook on HIGH heat setting for 2 to 4 hours.

2. For Crumble Topping, 30 minutes before fruit is ready, preheat oven to 350 degrees F. Line a baking sheet with aluminum foil; set aside.

3. In a medium bowl, stir together granola, baking mix, gingersnaps, and melted butter. Spread evenly on prepared baking sheet. Bake in preheated oven for 12 to 18 minutes or until crisp and golden.

4. To serve, spoon half of the Slow-Cooked Cherries into dessert dishes. Sprinkle with half of the Crumble Topping. Top each serving with a scoop of ice cream. Spoon on remaining Slow-Cooked Cherries and sprinkle with remaining Crumble Topping.

Deep-Dish
Ginger-Peach Pie

Prep 20 minutes
Cook LOW 4 to 5 hours
Makes 10 servings

1	box (15-ounce) rolled refrigerated unbaked piecrusts, *Pillsbury*® (2 crusts)
	Butter-flavor cooking spray, *Mazola® Pure*
2	cans (21 ounces each) peach pie filling, *Comstock® More Fruit*
¾	cup packed brown sugar, *C&H*®
1¼	teaspoons ground ginger, *McCormick*®
1	teaspoon ground cinnamon, *McCormick*®
1	container (15-ounce) ricotta cheese, *Precious*®
1	large egg, slightly beaten
⅓	cup granulated sugar
¼	cup crystallized ginger, chopped finely, *McCormick*®

1. Let piecrust stand at room temperature according to package directions. Lightly coat a 5-quart slow cooker with cooking spray; set aside.

2. In a medium bowl, combine pie filling, ½ cup of the brown sugar, ¾ teaspoon of the ground ginger, and ½ teaspoon of the cinnamon. Set aside.

3. In another medium bowl, whisk together ricotta cheese, egg, granulated sugar, and crystallized ginger; set aside.

4. Unroll 1 piecrust and fit into the bottom of prepared slow cooker. Spread half of the ricotta cheese mixture onto piecrust. Top with all of the peach mixture. Top with remaining ricotta mixture. Top with remaining piecrust, tucking edges of crust down sides of slow cooker. Cut a slit in the top to allow steam to escape. Sprinkle with remaining brown sugar, ground ginger, and cinnamon. Stack 8 paper towels. Place on top of slow cooker (to absorb moisture). Secure with lid.

5. Cook on LOW heat setting for 4 to 5 hours. Uncover slow cooker; remove paper towels. Cool 2 hours at room temperature. Chill pie overnight, uncovered, in the slow cooker.* Slice to serve.

*Note: The pie is chilled overnight so it is easier to slice into uniform pieces and remove from the slow cooker. If you would like to serve the pie sooner, it can be spooned from the slow cooker after cooling at room temperature for at least 2 hours.

White Chocolate-Cranberry Bread Pudding

Prep 15 minutes
Cook LOW 3 to 4 hours
Makes 6 servings

	Butter-flavor cooking spray, *Mazola® Pure*
1	loaf (16-ounce) Texas toast (thick-sliced bread), cut into 1-inch cubes*
1	bag (12-ounce) white chocolate pieces
1	cup dried cranberries, *Ocean Spray®*
3	large eggs
1	cup milk
1	cup heavy cream
½	cup sugar
	Dash salt
2	tablespoons butter, cut into small pieces
1	teaspoon ground cinnamon, *McCormick®*
	Chocolate-flavored syrup, *Hershey's®*

1. Coat a 4-quart slow cooker with cooking spray.

2. In a large bowl, toss together bread cubes, white chocolate pieces, and cranberries until combined.

3. In a medium bowl, whisk together eggs, milk, cream, sugar, and salt. Pour over bread mixture. Stir together. Transfer to prepared slow cooker. Dot with butter and sprinkle with cinnamon.

4. Cover and cook on LOW heat setting for 3 to 4 hours.

5. Serve warm with chocolate-flavored syrup.

*Note: Bread is easier to cube if slightly stale.

Indian Pudding

Prep 15 minutes
Cook HIGH 1 hour; plus 2 hours on LOW
Makes 8 servings

Adding butterscotch pudding and corn muffin mix, instead of cornmeal, gives Indian Pudding a sweeter taste. Try it the traditional way, with a scoop of vanilla ice cream melting on top of each hot-from-the-pot serving.

	Butter-flavor cooking spray, *Mazola® Pure*
1	**box (8.5-ounce) instant corn muffin mix, *Jiffy®***
1	**box (3.4-ounce) instant butterscotch pudding and pie filling mix, *Jell-O®***
6	**cups milk**
3	**large eggs**
½	**cup dark or robust molasses, *Grandma's®***
1	**teaspoon ground cinnamon, *McCormick®***
½	**teaspoon ground ginger, *McCormick®***
	Crumbled sugar cookies (optional)

1. Coat a 4-quart slow cooker with cooking spray; set aside.

2. In a large bowl, whisk together corn muffin mix, pudding mix, and 3 cups of the milk for 2 to 3 minutes or until thickened; set aside.

3. In a medium bowl, lightly beat eggs with a whisk. Whisk in remaining milk, molasses, cinnamon, and ginger. Stir into pudding mixture until thoroughly combined. Transfer to prepared slow cooker.

4. Cover and cook on HIGH heat setting for 1 hour. Turn slow cooker to LOW heat setting; stir. Cover and cook for 1 hour. Stir; cover and cook for 1 hour more.

5. Serve warm topped with crumbled sugar cookies (optional).

Toasted Coconut Rice Pudding

Prep 15 minutes
Cook LOW 4 hours
Makes 8 servings

Butter-flavor cooking spray, *Mazola® Pure*
1 cup shredded coconut, *Baker's®*
1 can (14-ounce) coconut milk, *Thai Kitchen®*
1 can (14-ounce) sweetened condensed milk, *Carnation®*
4 large eggs
2 teaspoons bottled chopped ginger, *Christopher Ranch®*
2 bags (8.8 ounces each) long-grain ready rice, *Uncle Ben's®*
   Chopped fresh mango (optional)
   Chopped fresh papaya (optional)

1. Coat a 4-quart slow cooker with cooking spray; set aside. In a large skillet, over medium-high heat, cook and stir coconut until golden. Transfer skillet to a wire rack. Set aside 2 tablespoons of the toasted coconut (optional).

2. In a large bowl, whisk together coconut milk, condensed milk, eggs, and ginger. Stir in rice and the remaining toasted coconut. Pour into prepared slow cooker.

3. Cover and cook on LOW heat setting for 4 hours.

4. Serve with mango, papaya, and reserved toasted coconut (optional).

Carrot Spoon Cake

Prep 20 minutes
Cook LOW 4½ to 6 hours
Makes 10 servings

Butter-flavor cooking spray, *Mazola® Pure*
1   **box (18.25-ounce) spice cake mix, *Betty Crocker®***
2   **cups shredded carrots**
1   **box (3.4-ounce) instant butterscotch pudding and pie filling mix, *Jell-O®***
4   **large eggs**
1   **can (8-ounce) crushed pineapple, *Dole®***
1   **cup sour cream, *Knudsen®***
1   **cup water**
¾   **cup canola oil, *Wesson®***
    Heavy cream or whipped cream (optional)

1. Coat a 5-quart slow cooker with cooking spray.

2. In a large mixing bowl, combine cake mix, carrots, pudding mix, eggs, undrained pineapple, sour cream, water, and canola oil. Beat with a handheld electric mixer on medium speed for 2 minutes. Transfer to slow cooker.

3. Cover and cook on LOW heat setting for 4½ to 6 hours.

4. Serve warm with cream (optional).

Lemon-Blueberry Cake

Prep 20 minutes
Cook HIGH 2¼ to 2½ hours
Makes 10 servings

Butter-flavor cooking spray, *Mazola® Pure*
1 **can (21-ounce) blueberry pie filling,** *Comstock® More Fruit*
1 **box (18.25-ounce) lemon cake mix,** *Betty Crocker®*
1¼ **cups water**
⅓ **cup canola oil,** *Wesson®*
3 **large eggs**
1¼ **cups boiling water**
¼ **cup sugar**

1. Coat a 4½- or 5-quart slow cooker with cooking spray. Spoon pie filling into slow cooker; set aside.

2. In a large mixing bowl, combine cake mix, the 1¼ cups water, the canola oil, and eggs. Using a handheld electric mixer, beat on medium speed for 2 minutes, occasionally scraping side of bowl. Pour over pie filling in slow cooker.

3. In a medium bowl, combine the 1¼ cups boiling water and the sugar, stirring to dissolve sugar. Slowly pour sugar-water mixture over cake batter in slow cooker. Stack 8 paper towels. Place over the top of the slow cooker without touching the cake mix (to absorb moisture). Secure with cover.

4. Cook on HIGH heat setting for 2¼ to 2½ hours or until a wooden skewer inserted near the center comes out clean. Remove liner from slow cooker, if possible, or turn off slow cooker. Let stand, uncovered, for 30 to 45 minutes to cool slightly before serving.

5. Scoop cake onto dessert plates.* Serve warm topped with blueberry mixture left in bottom of cooker.

*Note: Cake can also be left to cool completely and sliced.

Chocolate-Peanut Butter Brownies

Prep 25 minutes
Cook HIGH 4 hours
Makes 10 servings

	Butter-flavor cooking spray, *Mazola® Pure*
3	**large eggs**
1	**box (19.8-ounce) brownie mix, *Betty Crocker®***
$\frac{1}{2}$	**cup vegetable oil, *Wesson®***
$\frac{1}{4}$	**cup water**
$\frac{1}{2}$	**cup creamy peanut butter, *Skippy®***
1	**tablespoon packed brown sugar, *C&H®***
	Whipped cream (optional)

1. Coat a 6-cup soufflé dish with cooking spray; set aside.

2. In a large bowl, beat 2 of the eggs with a whisk. Whisk in brownie mix, vegetable oil, and water until thoroughly combined. Transfer to prepared soufflé dish.

3. In a medium bowl, beat remaining egg with a whisk. Whisk in peanut butter and brown sugar. Drop mixture by spoonfuls over brownie mix mixture. Using a table knife, cut peanut butter mixture through brownie mix mixture to create a marbling effect; set aside.

4. Crumple aluminum foil to create a "ring base" about 5 inches in diameter and 1 inch thick. Place in a 5-quart slow cooker. Place soufflé dish on top of ring. Stack 8 paper towels; place over slow cooker (to absorb moisture). Secure with lid.

5. Cook on HIGH heat setting for 4 hours or until set.

6. Transfer soufflé dish to a wire rack; cool completely. Using a thin-bladed knife, loosen edge of brownies from dish. Invert onto a cutting board. Turn brownies again (so top is facing up) and slice.

7. Serve with whipped cream (optional).

Hot Cocoa Cake

Prep 20 minutes
Cook LOW 4 hours **Stand** 5 minutes
Makes 10 servings

Slow-cooked cake may be the most moist cake you'll ever eat. Chocolate pudding and scalded milk seep into the batter during baking, making the cake rich down to the crumbs. Melt marshmallows on top before serving.

	Butter-flavor cooking spray, *Mazola® Pure*
2	**cups milk**
1	**box (18.25-ounce) chocolate cake mix, *Betty Crocker®***
1¼	**cups water**
3	**large eggs**
⅓	**cup canola oil, *Wesson®***
1	**box (5-ounce) chocolate cook-and-serve pudding mix, *Jell-O®***
	Miniature marshmallows, *Kraft®*
	Chocolate-flavored syrup, *Hershey's®*

1. Coat a 5-quart slow cooker with cooking spray; set aside. In a small saucepan, over high heat, heat milk until almost boiling. Remove from heat; set aside.

2. In a large mixing bowl, combine cake mix, water, eggs, and canola oil. Using a handheld electric mixer, beat on medium speed for 2 minutes, occasionally scraping down side of bowl.

3. Transfer batter to prepared slow cooker. Sprinkle pudding mix over cake batter. Slowly pour in hot milk.

4. Cover and cook on LOW heat setting for 4 hours. (Do not lift lid for first 3 hours of cooking.)

5. Turn off slow cooker. Sprinkle cake with 1 cup of the marshmallows. Cover; let stand for 5 minutes to allow marshmallows to melt slightly.

6. Serve warm by scooping out cake.* Top with additional marshmallows and chocolate-flavored syrup (optional).

*Note: Cake also can be left to cool completely and sliced.

Index

Index

236

237

Free

Lifestyle web magazine subscription

Just visit
www.semi-homemade.com
today to subscribe!

Sign yourself and your friends and family up to the semi-homemaker's club today!

Each online issue is filled with fast, easy how-to projects, simple lifestyle solutions, and an abundance of helpful hints and terrific tips. It's the complete go-to magazine for busy people on-the-move.

tables & settings   fashion & beauty   ideas   home & garden   fabulous florals

super suppers   perfect parties   great gatherings   decadent desserts

gifts & giving   details   wines & music   fun favors   semi-homemaker's club

Semi-Homemade.com

making life easier, better, and more enjoyable

Semihomemade.com has hundreds of ways to simplify your life—the easy Semi-Homemade way! You'll find fast ways to de-clutter, try your hand at clever crafts, create terrific tablescapes or decorate indoors and out to make your home and garden superb with style.

We're especially proud of our Semi-Homemakers club: a part of semi-homemade.com which hosts other semihomemakers just like you. The club community shares ideas to make life easier, better, and more manageable with smart tips and hints allowing you time to do what you want! Sign-up and join today—it's free—and sign up your friends and family, too! It's easy the Semi-Homemade way! Visit the site today and start enjoying your busy life!

Sign yourself and your friends and family up to the semi-homemaker's club today!

tablescapes	home	garden	organizing	crafts
everyday & special days	cooking	entertaining	cocktail time	
Halloween	Thanksgiving	Christmas	Valentine's	Easter	New Year's

About Sandra Lee

Sandra Lee is a *New York Times* best-selling author and a nationally acclaimed lifestyle expert. Her signature Semi-Homemade approach to cooking, home decorating, gardening, crafting, entertaining, beauty, and fashion offers savvy shortcuts and down-to-earth secrets for creating a beautiful, affordable, and most importantly doable lifestyle.

Sandra Lee's cookbook series offers amazing meals in minutes, fabulous food fixin's, and sensational—yet simple—style ideas. *Semi-Homemade Cooking with Sandra Lee* is one of Food Network's hottest cooking shows, providing many helpful hints, timesaving techniques, tips, and tricks.

Find even more sensible, savvy solutions online at semihomemade.com.

Sandra Lee Semi-Homemade® Cookbook Series
Collect all these amazingly helpful, timesaving, and beautiful books!
Look for the series wherever quality books are sold.